EXCELLER
SELECT

TOP PICKS

The New Era of **LEADERLESS** *Leadership*

The New Era of

LEADERLESS

Leadership

Empowering Voices, Inspiring Change

Pastor Ben Ochieng, CPA

EXCELLER BOOKS®
A GLOBAL PRESS

The New Era of Leaderless Leadership
Empowering Voices, Inspiring Change

Cover by Exceller Books using resources from Pixabay.com

ISBN: 978-93-48892-13-3

First published in India in 2025 by Exceller Books,
An imprint of GE Group
Address: G1, Dream Apartment, Degree College Road, Belgharia,
Kolkata, 700056, India
www.excellerbooks.com

EXCELLER BOOKS®
A GLOBAL PRESS

Dedication

To my family and friends, whose unwavering support and belief in me have been my guiding light.

To my mentor and foster father, Rev. CPA Kiganane Mulusa of Compassion International; and King Jesus Faith Ministries International, Nairobi City Centre Church, whose wisdom and encouragement have been invaluable.

To all the unsung heroes who believe in the power of collective wisdom and the strength of unity.

This book is for those who lead without titles, inspire without recognition, and harness the true potential of a decentralized world. Your courage and vision light the path for a brighter, more inclusive future.

In the tapestry of life, your threads of guidance and love have woven the fabric of my journey. May this work be a testament to the boundless potential within each of us, when we come together as one.

ACKNOWLEDGEMENT

Writing this book has been a journey of discovery, growth, and collaboration. I am deeply grateful to everyone who has supported me along the way.

I am indebted to all my colleagues and peers who have shared their knowledge and experiences with me, including those who have written their endorsements. Your contributions have enriched this book in countless ways.

I extend my deepest gratitude to my esteemed friend, Counsel Anthony Leshan, for his exceptional generosity in agreeing to write the foreword for *The Leaderless Leader*. Your unwavering support and belief in my work have been a source of immense encouragement and inspiration.

Anthony, your profound wisdom and dedication to the principles of leadership have significantly influenced my journey. I recall a particular instance when your guidance was invaluable—during a challenging period in my investment journey, which is also when and where we first met. Your insightful advice and steadfast support helped me navigate uncertainty and emerge with renewed clarity and purpose. This personal experience is a testament to your remarkable character and the strength of our friendship.

Your piece, "Change is the only constant in life," attributed to the Greek philosopher Heraclitus, is a perfect fit. It's like you read my mind—or maybe you just have a remarkable knack for knowing exactly what's needed. Either way, I'm grateful, Counsel! As they say, "A good friend will help you move, but a best friend will help you move a body." Thankfully, your contribution was far more valuable! Your insights on leadership are like a secret recipe—everyone wants to know it, but only a few can truly master it. I count myself among the most fortunate to tap into this tapestry of wisdom.

Remember that time we didn't know what to do in the aforementioned investment mix? Just like then, your sense of direction—both literal and metaphorical—has always been spot on. And who could forget the time you turned a high-stakes meeting into a masterclass on leadership with your quick thinking and humor? Your friendship has been a guiding light, even as we navigated the most unexpected detours.

To add a touch of divine blessing, let me share this scripture with you: "The Lord bless you and keep you; the Lord make his face shine on you and be gracious to you; the Lord turn his face toward you and give you peace." – *Numbers 6:24-26*

As a humorous leadership quote goes, "Leadership is the art of getting someone else to do something you want done because he wants to do it." – *Dwight D. Eisenhower* Your ability to inspire and lead is truly remarkable. And just for fun: "Goats are like mushrooms. If you shoot a duck, I'm scared of toasters." – *Unknown.* Because sometimes, leadership feels just as random!

The Leaderless Leader explores the transformative power of decentralized leadership, emphasizing the importance of collective decision-making, empowerment, and the strength found in diverse perspectives. Your willingness to lend your voice to this project is a testament to your good heart and the strength of our friendship. Your presence in this endeavor means more to me than words can express.

As John Quincy Adams once said, "If your actions inspire others to dream more, learn more, do more and become more, you are a leader." Anthony, you embody this quote in every sense, and I am honored to have you contribute to this book. With heartfelt appreciation—thank you!

A special thanks to my editor, Ms. Anjita Ganguly, Co-founder and Publication Expert, and to the Publishing Team at Exceller Books, for your meticulous attention to detail and your unwavering commitment to excellence. Your feedback has been instrumental in refining this work. And for patiently dealing with my endless drafts and occasional existential crises—you're a true star in the publishing industry!

To the countless individuals who have inspired me with their stories of leadership and resilience, this book is a testament to your courage and vision. Your experiences have shown me the true power of collective wisdom and the strength of unity.

To the GenZs in every corner of the globe—the African GenZs from across the continent, particularly in Kenya, South Africa, Nigeria, Mozambique, and during the Arab Spring, as well as those in Europe, the Americas, Bangladesh, and the larger Asia—thank you for providing alternative leadership away from the traditional centers of power. Your courage and innovative approaches have shown the world the strength of decentralized leadership and the power of bold, collective action. Your resilience, even in the face of grave danger, has brought a sense of sanity to leadership. Despite many being gunned down, going missing, or being abducted, your unwavering spirit has paid off and continues to pave the way for a brighter future.

Finally, to my readers, thank you for embarking on this journey with me. I hope this book inspires you to harness the power of collective leadership and to make a positive impact in your communities and beyond. And to my learned friends—should you find any typos, let's just call them "Easter eggs" for your amusement! Remember, perfection is overrated. It's the "quirks" that make life interesting.

Pastor Ben Ochieng, CPA
Kenya

KEY THEMES OF THE BOOK

- *Servant Leadership:* Emphasizing the importance of leading by serving others, inspired by biblical principles such as *Matthew 20:26.*
- *Empowerment and Collaboration:* How empowering team members and fostering collaboration can lead to greater innovation and success.
- *Decentralized Decision-Making:* The benefits of distributing decision-making power to create more agile and responsive organizations.
- *Moral and Ethical Leadership:* The role of strong moral values in guiding leaders and their teams through complex challenges.
- *Community and Collective Power:* Building a sense of community and harnessing the collective power of a group to achieve common goals.

Pastor Ben's engaging writing style, combined with his deep faith and professional experience, *makes this book a must-read* for anyone looking to lead effectively in a decentralized world. His insights are both profound and practical, offering readers a roadmap to harnessing *the power of collective leadership.*

Key Quotes

1. "True leadership is not about titles or positions, but about empowering others to find their own path."
2. "In a world where everyone wants to lead, the true leader is the one who serves." - Inspired by Matthew 20:26
3. "The strength of a community lies in its ability to harness the collective power of its members."
4. "Decentralized leadership is about trust and collaboration, not control and command."
5. "Empowerment is the cornerstone of effective leadership in a decentralized world."
6. "Moral and ethical leadership is the compass that guides us through the complexities of modern life."
7. "A leader's greatest success is measured by the growth and empowerment of those they lead."
8. "In the balance of power, it is the collective effort that tips the scales towards greatness."
9. "Leadership is not a solo journey; it is a collective endeavor that thrives on shared vision and mutual respect."

"The essence of leadership is not in being the loudest voice, but in being the most supportive presence."

Table of Contents

Part 6: The Future of Leaderless Leadership

Part 7: A New Dawn

Appendices

ENDORSEMENTS

"As a Seasoned Lawyer, I've seen leadership in many forms. CPA Ben, a work colleague and Pastor, blends faith, finance, and leadership into a tapestry of wisdom. His book, *'The New Era of Leaderless Leadership,'* is a game-changer. Ben's example of the Linux Open Source Project, where programmers worldwide collaborate without a central authority, is both inspiring and amusing. He quips, *'Trying to lead without listening is like trying to herd cats – you might get somewhere, but it won't be where you intended!'* Reflecting on my own experiences, I see the power of collective action.

Matthew 18:20 reminds us, 'For where two or three gather in my name, there am I with them.' Ben's insights will inspire you to rethink leadership and embrace the strength in unity - 'The Power of Us: Fostering Creativity Through Collaborative Leadership Over Chaotic Commands and Control!'" May we all not only read but also apply these principles both in faith and action for a better society!
– Jacky Akinyi, Legal Senior, Crowe Erastus & Co., Nairobi, Kenya.

"The Leaderless Leadership" is an exceptional exploration of decentralized leadership that challenges traditional notions of power and authority. The *book beautifully* intertwines historical insights, real-world applications, and ethical considerations to present a *compelling case* for inclusive and collaborative decision-making. The author's engaging narrative and practical strategies make this work not just a book but a *guide for navigating the complexities of modern leadership.*

One quote that resonated deeply with me was, *"The best leader is the one who has sense enough to pick good men (and women) to do what (s)he wants done, and self-restraint enough to keep from meddling with them while they do it"* (Theodore Roosevelt, referenced in the book). This quote compresses the essence of the book's philosophy: That true leadership lies in empowering others and trusting in their capabilities.

The book's practical insights and examples, such as the transformative power of leaderless movements, illustrate how this approach can create stronger, more innovative teams. It challenges readers to *rethink leadership not as control but as collaboration*, showing

how shared purpose can unlock extraordinary potential. This book is more than just an exploration of leadership — *it's a manifesto for building a better future.* It inspires hope and provides tools for those who want to lead with courage, compassion, and a commitment to collective progress. I highly recommend this book to anyone seeking to lead with authenticity and purpose.
– Lieutenant Colonel Salim Wamukoya, KDF, Directing Staff, Joint Command and Staff College, Karen, Nairobi Kenya.

The Leaderless Leader by Pastor Ben is a unique and insightful book that explores a path not often travelled. The author skilfully highlights the collective desire to shape and influence our environments for a common, desired outcome. What sets this book apart is Pastor Ben's approach to leadership, which emphasizes collaboration, trust, and shared responsibility. His ability to organize his thoughts clearly and structure the concepts makes them easy to follow and understand.

I highly recommend this book to anyone seeking a fresh perspective on leadership—one that a single individual does not drive but rather by the collective efforts and trust of leaders and followers alike.
– Eric M. Kirea, BA, MSC. Director, Christian Ministries in Africa (CMIA), and Associate Pastor, Church on The Rock, Langata, Nairobi, Kenya.

'The New Era of Leaderless Leadership' by CPA Ben is a *distinctive and penetrating* book that shows us a new era of leadership that we need to explore in our daily activities of running our departments, organizations, and society. CPA Ben has clearly stated the *conflict resolution mechanics* in a powerful way that if put into practice, then we will have a good world to live in.

I have *practised* some of these mechanics, like mediation, which have worked well. What makes this book unique is the author's ability to show how *equality, transparency, and accountability* can be applied in leadership to prevent misunderstanding among the various members and enhance innovation and problem-solving.

I highly recommend this book to anyone who wants to lead and is *inspired to change.*
– Ouko Stephen, BPS, MSc. MKISM, MCIPS, Procurement Officer. Also, Leader - ECCA Church, Kisumu Kenya.

A thought-provoking book, The New Era of Leaderless Leadership: Empowering Voices, Inspiring Change" gives the reader a glimpse into just how far leadership has metamorphosed.

A captivating read, CPA-Pastor Bernard's use of actual real-life national and global events such as the Black Lives Matter movement, #MeTooMovement, #OccupyParliament and #OccupyChurches, among others, to highlight specific points kept me engaged, making this book both relatable and practical.

Just as I found myself rethinking the impact of technology and social media on leadership, "The New Era of Leaderless Leadership" will provoke your thoughts and cause a mindset shift on the trajectory of leadership in years to come. This book is a definite must-read!

– Sharon Obwar, Audit Senior & Team Leader, Crowe Erastus & Co., Nairobi, Kenya.

Pastor Ben Ochieng's "The Leaderless Leader" is an insightful exploration of decentralized leadership, presenting a timely and innovative approach to modern governance, organizational dynamics, and societal change. The book advocates for a paradigm shift from traditional hierarchical models to a system that emphasizes inclusivity, collective decision-making, and the empowerment of all participants. It blends historical examples, real-world applications, and scriptural references to provide a holistic perspective on leaderless leadership.

Rich Historical Context: Pastor Ochieng enriches the narrative with historical and contemporary case studies, including the Occupy Wall Street movement, the #EndSARS protests, and the Linux Open Source Project. These examples effectively demonstrate the practical applications and successes of leaderless models.

Ethical Framework: The book delves into the ethical considerations of inclusivity, transparency, and trust. It challenges readers to uphold accountability and adopt collective responsibility, which resonates deeply with scriptural principles.

Practical Tools: Offering actionable strategies such as self-managing teams, consensus-building techniques, and conflict-resolution methods, the book equips readers with practical tools to implement leaderless leadership in various contexts.

Inspirational Tone: Incorporating scripture and personal anecdotes lends a motivational and relatable quality, making it informative and inspiring.

Clarity on Challenges: While the book highlights the challenges of leaderless leadership, such as decision-making inefficiencies and potential conflicts, a more detailed discussion on overcoming these hurdles in specific scenarios could add value.

Broader Industry Applications: Expanding on how leaderless leadership principles can be tailored to diverse industries or global contexts could make the book more universally applicable.

Visual Aids: Charts, diagrams, or infographics summarizing key concepts and frameworks could enhance reader engagement and comprehension.

"The Leaderless Leader" is a transformative work that redefines leadership for the 21st century. Its emphasis on collaboration, innovation, and ethical decision-making positions it as a guide for leaders and organizations striving for inclusivity and resilience. Pastor Ochieng has masterfully articulated a vision for a decentralized future where every voice matters. I commend the author for this groundbreaking contribution and encourage further exploration of these ideas in future works.

– *CPA Andrew Bulemi, Managing Partner, CEO, Mbaya & Associates Certified Public Accountants, Nairobi Kenya*

FOREWORD

Change is the only constant in life', a famous quote attributed to the Greek Philosopher Heraclitus, rings true in every aspect of our lives.

The world we live in keeps changing minute by minute, in multiple perspectives, fast, sometimes furiously.

In circumstances where change is constant, *challenges abound*, making the need for effective leadership more critical than ever in an *increasingly interconnected world.*

As a dispute resolution practitioner, I encounter clients with myriad legal challenges that need resolution.

Some of the matters that come to my desk may be simple and easily resolvable, others high stakes complex disputes, including those that implicate the laws of multiple jurisdictions, different business and legal cultures, or those that raise novel legal issues which existing domestic or international legal frameworks may not adequately address.

Some disputes involve individuals and families; others include societies, corporations, not-for-profit organizations, governments, and government agencies.

As a matter of fact, I came to meet CPA Benard Ochieng in November 2023 in the context of a complex commercial dispute involving an investment company and over 3000 investors.

The company owed investors a colossal USD 106,463,877/- (equivalent to KES 14 billion) and was in a situation where it was unable to pay the debt. Numerous court cases have been filed against the company. Investors were baying for blood, infuriated by the company's inability to pay them back. The winding up of the company was imminent, and so was the possibility of a total loss of investor funds.

A seven-member committee had been set up by the company investors to pursue stabilisation of the situation and resolution of the matter, with Benard as one of its members. The Committee then engaged me as its legal advisor.

As legal advisor to the Committee, I saw firsthand the transformative power of decentralized collaborative leadership and collective decision-making.

The Committee, through engagements with the investor base as well as other stakeholders, has been able to achieve a *modicum* of stability that has safeguarded the company's assets portfolio from wastage and preserved them for the benefit of investors. What they have been on can *aptly* be described as a 'rescue operation', one that will likely ultimately facilitate the repayment of the principal sums to the investors. Impact!

Benard's role in the Committee has been pivotal. Right from his ability to assess the problem, to engaging stakeholders in crafting a solution, from building genuine relationships with his team members to regularly checking in on them to see what's happening and what's not and to encouraging them through the challenging task, Benard's leadership style is admirable and is an inspiration to many.

He is uniquely qualified to write a book on leadership. This book is a timely guide for anyone seeking to understand the fundamentals of impactful leadership. It provides insights to anyone seeking to develop their leadership abilities, and provides a framework which individuals, families, societies, corporates, organizations and indeed governments and government agencies may work with to navigate complex situations, inspire teamwork, and achieve impactful results.

CPA Benard Ochieng has *distilled* years of experience in leadership in both corporate and religious settings into a practical framework for leaders and aspiring leaders in all spheres that is bound to provide them with the foundation on which to lead with purpose and impact.

As you negotiate your way in this ever-changing world and through the endless challenges it brings, I am confident that this book will be a *reliable anchor*, providing you with the tools to marshal and work with human collaborators to achieve your goals and to intensify impact in the world.

Anthony Leshan
Advocate of the High Court of the Republic of Kenya

Introduction

"The best leader is the one who has sense enough to pick good men (and women) to do what he wants done, and self-restraint enough to keep from meddling with them while they do it."

— Theodore Roosevelt

- *The Concept of Leaderless Leadership*

In a world where traditional hierarchies and centralized power structures have long dominated, the concept of leaderless leadership emerges as a revolutionary approach. Leaderless leadership refers to a form of organization where decision-making and authority are distributed among all members rather than centralized in a single leader. This model challenges the conventional wisdom that effective leadership requires a singular, authoritative figure at the helm. Instead, it promotes a more democratic, inclusive, and collaborative approach to leadership.

- *Historical Context and Evolution*

The roots of leaderless leadership can be traced back to various social and political movements throughout history. One notable example is the leaderless resistance movements of the 20th century, which operated without a central command to avoid detection and suppression by authorities. These movements demonstrated the power of decentralized organizations in achieving significant social and political change.

In more recent times, the Occupy Wall Street movement, which began in 2011, exemplifies the principles of leaderless leadership. Protesters organized large-scale demonstrations to protest economic inequality and corporate influence on government, all without a central leadership figure. This movement highlighted the potential of collective action and the power of a shared vision to drive change.

- *Relevance in Today's World*

In today's rapidly changing and interconnected world, leaderless leadership offers a viable alternative to traditional leadership models. The rise of digital communication tools and social media platforms has made it easier for individuals to collaborate and organize without the need for a central authority. This shift is particularly relevant in the context of the gig economy, remote work, and globalized networks, where flexibility and adaptability are paramount.

Leaderless leadership empowers individuals by giving them a voice and a stake in the decision-making process. It fosters innovation by encouraging diverse perspectives and ideas. Moreover, it promotes resilience, as decentralized organizations are often more adaptable and responsive to change than their hierarchical counterparts.

- *Real-World Applications*

To illustrate the power and potential of leaderless leadership, consider the following real-world examples:

- Kenya's Gen Z Protests (2024): In June 2024, young Kenyans organized leaderless protests against opulence among top government officials and the Finance Bill 2024, which proposed significant tax hikes on basic commodities. These protests were largely coordinated through social media platforms and were marked by their decentralized nature. The movement quickly spread to other African countries like Uganda, Nigeria, and Mozambique, where young people also protested against electoral malpractices, bad governance, and economic hardships (Hivos, 2024; The Africa Report, 2024).

  Hivos is an international organization that works towards creating just, inclusive, and life-sustaining societies. In 2024, Hivos continues to focus on its Strategic Compass 2021-2024, which aims to bring more focus to their programs, restructure the organization, and find solutions for eroding public trust in institutions1. This strategy aligns with the international agenda set through 2030, including the Sustainable Development Goals (SDGs) and the principle of "leaving no one behind". Additionally, Hivos' R.O.O.M. program (Resources of Open Minds) has been empowering creators across Africa and the Middle East to amplify diverse, alternative ethical and social narratives2. This program aims to challenge the status quo and support creative solutions to societal issues.

The Africa Report is a publication that provides in-depth analysis and insights on various political, economic, and social issues across the African continent. In 2024, it covers a range of topics, including:

1. *Elections:* Several African countries, such as South Africa and Ghana, are holding significant elections.
2. *Economic Challenges:* The report discusses the rising debt levels in many African countries and the associated economic challenges.
3. *Political Developments:* Key political events and changes, including South Africa's critical election, are highlighted.
4. *Social Issues:* The report also addresses social issues like inflation, poverty, and food insecurity.

- #EndSARS Movement in Nigeria: Although it began in 2020, the #EndSARS movement continued to influence protests in Nigeria through 2023. This movement, which called for the disbandment of the Special Anti-Robbery Squad (SARS) due to police brutality, was largely leaderless and driven by social media activism (Hivos, 2024).
- Hong Kong Protests: The protests in Hong Kong, which began in 2019, continued to have an impact through 2023. These protests were characterized by their decentralized organization, with no single leader

or group directing the movement. Protesters used social media and encrypted messaging apps to coordinate their actions and maintain momentum (Hivos, 2024).

- Farmers' Protests in India (2020-2021): Although the main protests occurred earlier, the impact of the farmers' protests in India continued to be felt in 2023. These protests were against three farm laws and were marked by their decentralized nature, with farmers from different states coming together without a central leadership (Hivos, 2024).
- The Occupy Wall Street Movement: This movement, which began in 2011, aimed to protest economic inequality and the influence of corporations on government. Despite having no central leadership, the movement managed to organize large-scale protests and gain significant media attention. This example demonstrates how leaderless leadership can mobilize people around a common cause and drive social change.
- The Linux Open Source Project: Developed through a collaborative effort by programmers around the world, Linux operates without a central authority. Contributors work together to improve the software, guided by a shared vision and set of principles. This example highlights the potential of leaderless leadership to foster innovation and create high-quality products.
- The Zapatista Movement: The Zapatista Army of National Liberation (EZLN) in Mexico operates on principles of leaderless leadership. The movement emphasizes collective decision-making and community autonomy, challenging traditional power structures. This example underscores the importance of inclusivity and equal participation in leaderless leadership.

- Lebanon and Iraq Protests (2019-2020): Both Lebanon and Iraq experienced massive, leaderless protests driven by frustration with corruption, economic inequality, and lack of basic services. These movements were characterized by their decentralized nature, with no single leader or group directing the actions.
- Chile Protests (2019): In Chile, widespread protests erupted over economic inequality and the high cost of living. The movement was largely leaderless, with various groups and individuals organizing demonstrations through social media.
- Thailand Protests (2020-2021): The youth-led protests in Thailand called for democratic reforms and the resignation of the prime minister. These protests were organized without a central leadership, relying on social media to coordinate actions and spread their message

Imagine a group of friends deciding to start a community garden. Instead of appointing a leader, they all agree to share responsibilities equally. Each person brings their unique skills to the table; one is great at organizing events, another has a green thumb, and another excels at fundraising. Together, they create a thriving garden that becomes a hub for the community. This story illustrates how leaderless leadership can harness the collective strengths of a group to achieve a common goal.

Or picture a group of tech enthusiasts trying to build a robot. Without a designated leader, they initially struggle to agree on the design. One person suggests making it look like a cat, another insists on a dog, and yet another wants a dinosaur. After much debate (and laughter), they decide to create a multi-functional robot that can transform into all three. This humorous scenario highlights the creative potential of leaderless collaboration.

Matthew 18:20 (NIV) states, "For where two or three gather in my name, there am I with them." This scripture resonates deeply with the theme of leaderless leadership and the overall discussion in this book for several reasons, and underscores the power of collective action and the presence of a guiding spirit in group endeavors, resonating with the principles of leaderless leadership, as follows:

- *Collective Action and Presence:*

The verse emphasizes the power and presence that comes from collective action. In the context of leaderless leadership, it underscores the idea that significant impact and guidance can emerge from a group of individuals working together towards a common goal, even without a central leader. This aligns with the concept that leadership and inspiration can come from within the group itself.

- *Inclusivity and Collaboration:*

Leaderless leadership promotes inclusivity and collaboration, where every member's voice is valued and contributes to the decision-making process. Matthew 18:20 highlights the importance of gathering and working together, reinforcing the idea that collective efforts are powerful and meaningful.

- *Empowerment and Shared Responsibility:*

The scripture suggests that when individuals come together with a shared purpose, they are empowered and supported. This mirrors the principles of leaderless leadership, where authority and responsibility are distributed among all members, fostering a sense of ownership and empowerment.

- *Spiritual and Ethical Foundations:*

The verse provides a spiritual and ethical foundation for leaderless leadership. It suggests that a higher presence or guiding spirit is with those who gather and work together in unity. This can be seen as a metaphor for the collective wisdom and moral compass that guides leaderless movements and organizations.

- *Real-World Applications:*

In the real-world examples discussed above, such as the Occupy Wall Street movement, the #EndSARS protests, and the Gen Z protests in Kenya, the power of collective action without a central leader is evident. These movements demonstrate how groups of individuals can come together to drive significant social and political change, resonating with the message of Matthew 18:20.

By incorporating this scripture, the book highlights the spiritual and ethical dimensions of leaderless leadership, reinforcing the idea that collective action, inclusivity, and shared responsibility are not only effective but also deeply meaningful and guided by a higher purpose.

- *Application to Corporate Settings*

Leaderless Leadership in Corporate Settings:

1. Self-Managing Teams: In corporate settings, leaderless leadership can be implemented through self-managing teams. These teams operate without a designated leader, with members collectively making decisions and sharing responsibilities. This approach can foster a sense of ownership and accountability among team members.
2. Matrix Organizations: Matrix organizations involve multiple layers of management and reporting lines, encouraging collaboration across departments. This structure allows for shared leadership, where team members take on leadership roles based on their expertise and the specific needs of the project.
3. Flat Organizations: Flat organizations minimize hierarchical structures, promoting a more collaborative and inclusive work environment. In such setups, authority is decentralized, empowering

every team member to contribute their expertise and make decisions collectively.

4. Innovation and Adaptability: Leaderless leadership can drive innovation and adaptability in corporate settings. By encouraging diverse perspectives and ideas, organizations can foster a culture of creativity and continuous improvement.
5. Challenges in Corporate Settings: Despite its benefits, leaderless leadership in corporate settings can face challenges such as coordination difficulties, potential for conflict, and the need for clear frameworks for roles, communication, and conflict resolution.

- *Challenges of Leaderless Leadership*

1. Lack of Direction: Without a central leader, it can be challenging to establish a clear direction and unified goals. This can lead to confusion and inefficiency as members may have different interpretations of the movement's objectives.
2. Communication Breakdown: Effective communication is crucial for any organization. In leaderless movements, the absence of a central figure to facilitate communication can result in misunderstandings and fragmented messaging.
3. Decision-Making Difficulties: Leaderless movements often struggle with decision-making processes. Without a clear decision-making authority, reaching consensus can be time-consuming and contentious.
4. Frustration and Conflict: The lack of a clear leader can lead to frustration among members, especially when disagreements arise. This can result in internal conflicts and hinder the movement's progress.
5. Vulnerability to Co-optation: Leaderless movements can be vulnerable to co-optation by external forces. Without a central leadership to guard against such

influences, the movement's goals and actions can be easily manipulated.

- *Conclusion*

As we embark on this exploration of leaderless leadership, we will delve into its mechanics, ethical considerations, and real-world applications. We will examine how this model can transform organizations, movements, and societies by harnessing the collective power of individuals. Through case studies, personal anecdotes, and practical strategies, we will uncover the potential of leaderless leadership to create a more inclusive, innovative, and resilient world.

It presents both opportunities and challenges. While it can empower individuals, foster innovation, and create more inclusive environments, it also requires careful management to address potential issues such as lack of direction, communication breakdowns, and decision-making difficulties. In corporate settings, adopting leaderless leadership models like self-managing teams, matrix organizations, and flat structures can drive adaptability and creativity, but organizations must establish clear frameworks to ensure effective collaboration and conflict resolution.

Let's begin this journey together, embracing the possibilities of a decentralized future where every voice matters and collective action drives meaningful change.

Part 1:

Understanding Leaderless Leadership

"A leader is best when people barely know (s)he exists, when his / her work is done, his / her aim fulfilled, they will say: we did it ourselves."

— *Lao Tzu*

CHAPTER 1:
The Paradigm Shift

- *Traditional Leadership vs. Leaderless Leadership*

Traditional leadership models are characterized by hierarchical structures where authority and decision-making power are concentrated at the top. In contrast, leaderless leadership distributes these responsibilities among all members, fostering a more democratic and inclusive environment. This shift challenges the notion that effective leadership requires a singular, authoritative figure. As *John C. Maxwell* famously said, "A leader is one who knows the way, goes the way, and shows the way." In leaderless leadership, everyone is encouraged to find and show the way together.

➢ *Case Studies of Successful Leaderless Movements*

- *Occupy Wall Street:* This movement, which began in 2011, aimed to protest economic inequality and corporate influence on government. Despite lacking a central leadership figure, the movement organized large-scale protests and gained significant media attention. The decentralized structure allowed for diverse voices and ideas to shape the movement's direction.
- *The Arab Spring:* It was a series of anti-government protests and uprisings across the Arab world in the early 2010s. These movements were largely leaderless, relying on social media and grassroots organizing to mobilize people. The lack of a central authority made it difficult for regimes to suppress the movements, highlighting the power of collective action.
- *The Linux Open Source Project:* Developed through a collaborative effort by programmers around the world, Linux operates without a central authority.

Contributors work together to improve the software, guided by a shared vision and set of principles. This model has led to the creation of a robust and widely used operating system.

- *Benefits and Challenges*

- *Benefits*
    - ✓ *Inclusivity:* Leaderless leadership promotes equal participation, ensuring all voices are heard. As Simon Sinek puts it, "A boss has the title, the leader has the people".
    - ✓ *Innovation:* Diverse perspectives and ideas can lead to more creative solutions.
    - ✓ *Resilience:* Decentralized organizations are often more adaptable and responsive to change.

- *Challenges*
    - ✓ *Decision-Making:* Without a central authority, reaching a consensus can be time-consuming and difficult.
    - ✓ *Accountability:* Distributing responsibility can sometimes lead to a diffusion of accountability.
    - ✓ *Conflict Resolution:* Resolving conflicts without a clear leader can be complex.

CHAPTER 2:
The Psychology of Leaderless Leadership

- *Human Behavior in Leaderless Environments*

Understanding human behavior in leaderless environments is crucial for fostering effective collaboration. People are naturally inclined to seek structure and guidance, which can make the transition to a leaderless model challenging. However, with the right mind-set and tools, individuals can thrive in such environments. As *Peter Drucker* said, "Management is doing things right; leadership is doing the right things."

- *The Role of Trust and Collaboration*

Trust is the foundation of leaderless leadership. Without a central authority, members must rely on each other to fulfill their roles and responsibilities. Building trust requires open communication, transparency, and a commitment to shared goals. Collaboration is also key, as it allows members to leverage their collective strengths and expertise. "Trust is the glue of life. It's an essential ingredient in effective communication. It's the foundational principle that holds all relationships" (*Stephen R. Covey*).

- *Overcoming the Fear of Chaos*

One of the biggest challenges of leaderless leadership is overcoming the fear of chaos. Without a clear leader, there is a risk of disorganization and inefficiency. However, by establishing clear protocols, fostering a culture of trust, and leveraging technology, leaderless organizations can maintain order and achieve their goals. "Chaos is inherent in all compounded things. Strive on with diligence" (*Buddha*).

- *Real-World Applications and Personal Anecdotes*

- *The Arab Spring:* The Arab Spring is a powerful example of leaderless leadership in action. In countries like Tunisia and Egypt, citizens organized protests and uprisings without a central leadership figure. Social media plays a crucial role in mobilizing people and spreading information. This decentralized approach made it difficult for regimes to suppress the movements, ultimately leading to significant political change.
- *Personal Anecdote:* Imagine a group of students working on a group project. Instead of appointing a leader, they decide to share responsibilities equally. Each student takes on a task that aligns with their strengths, and they regularly meet to discuss progress and make decisions together. Despite initial challenges, they find that this collaborative approach leads to a more innovative and well-rounded project.
- *Humorous Story:* Picture a group of friends planning a surprise party. Without a designated leader, they initially struggle to agree on the theme. One person suggests a beach party, another wants a superhero theme, and another proposes a masquerade ball. After much debate (and laughter), they decide to combine all three themes into a unique and unforgettable party. This humorous scenario highlights the creative potential of leaderless collaboration.

- *Scriptural Reference*

"Two are better than one, because they have a good return for their labor: If either of them falls down, one can help the other up." (Ecclesiastes 4:9-10, NIV). This scripture emphasizes the power of collaboration and mutual support, which are essential components of leaderless leadership.

By understanding the paradigm shift and the psychology behind leaderless leadership and learning from real-world applications, we can appreciate the potential of this model to transform organizations and movements. Let's continue exploring the mechanics and ethical considerations of leaderless leadership in the next sections.

Part 2:

The Mechanics of Leaderless Leadership

"Leadership is not about being in charge. It is about taking care of those in your charge."

— Simon Sinek

CHAPTER 3:
Building a Leaderless Organization

- *Key Principles and Values*

Building a leaderless organization requires a strong foundation of principles and values that guide the group's actions and decisions. These principles include:

- *Equality:* Every member has an equal voice and the opportunity to contribute to decision-making processes. This principle ensures that all members feel valued and empowered, fostering a sense of ownership and responsibility.
- *Transparency:* Open communication and access to information are essential to build trust and ensure everyone is informed. Transparency helps prevent misunderstandings and promotes accountability.
- *Collaboration:* Collaboration means working together towards common goals, leveraging the diverse skills and perspectives of all members. Collaboration encourages innovation and problem-solving by bringing together different viewpoints.
- *Accountability:* While leadership is distributed, accountability must be clear. Each member is responsible for their actions and contributions, ensuring that the organization functions effectively.

- *Structuring for Success*

Creating a successful, leaderless organization involves careful planning and structuring. Here are some steps to consider:

- *Define Roles and Responsibilities:* Clearly outline the roles and responsibilities of each member to ensure accountability and prevent overlap. This clarity helps members understand their contributions and how they fit into the larger picture.

- *Establish Decision-Making Processes:* Develop processes for making decisions, such as consensus-building techniques or voting systems. These processes should be transparent and inclusive, allowing all members to participate.
- *Create Communication Channels:* Set up effective communication channels to facilitate open dialogue and information sharing. Tools like Slack or Microsoft Teams can help keep everyone connected and informed.
- *Implement Feedback Mechanisms:* Regularly solicit feedback from members to identify areas for improvement and ensure everyone feels heard. Feedback loops help the organization adapt and evolve based on member input.

▪ *Tools and Technologies that Facilitate Leaderless Leadership*

Leveraging the right tools and technologies can enhance the effectiveness of a leaderless organization. Some useful tools include:

- *Collaboration Platforms:* Tools like Slack, Microsoft Teams, and Trello can help facilitate communication and project management. These platforms allow for real-time collaboration and task tracking.
- *Decision-Making Tools:* Platforms like Loomio and Pol.is can assist in consensus-building and decision-making processes. These tools provide structured ways to gather input and make collective decisions.

Loomio is a flexible decision-making platform that helps groups create a more engaged and collaborative culture. It allows users to start discussion threads, use various types of polls (like dot voting and ranked choice), and make clear, transparent decisions together. It is particularly useful for organizations looking to streamline their decision processes and improve transparency and accountability.

Pol.is is an AI-powered conversation platform that helps groups, organizations, and authorities gather and analyze public opinion. Participants can add their opinions and vote on the opinions of others, creating a dynamic and inclusive conversation. This tool is often used to inform decision-making by capturing diverse perspectives and identifying common ground.

Both tools aim to make decision-making more inclusive and efficient by leveraging technology to gather input and build consensus.

- *Document Sharing:* Google Drive and Dropbox allow for easy sharing and collaboration of documents and files. These tools ensure that all members have access to the latest information and can contribute to shared documents.
- *Virtual Meeting Tools:* Zoom and Microsoft Teams enable remote collaboration and regular check-ins. These tools are essential for maintaining communication and coordination in a distributed organization.

CHAPTER 4:

Decision-Making Processes

- *Consensus-Building Techniques*

Consensus-building is a key aspect of leaderless leadership. Here are some techniques to consider:

- *Round-Robin Discussions:* Each member takes turns sharing their thoughts and opinions, ensuring everyone has a chance to speak. This technique helps prevent dominant voices from overshadowing others.
- *Dot Voting:* Members use dots to vote on different options, helping to visualize preferences and reach a consensus. This method is quick and visually clear, making it easy to see where the group's preferences lie.
- *Delphi Method:* This is a structured communication technique where members provide feedback through multiple rounds of questionnaires, gradually converging on a decision. This method is useful for complex decisions that require thorough consideration.

- *Conflict Resolution without a Central Authority*

Resolving conflicts in a leaderless organization requires clear processes and a commitment to collaboration. Here are some strategies:

- *Mediation:* Appoint neutral mediators to help facilitate discussions and resolve conflicts. Mediators can help ensure that all voices are heard and guide the group towards a resolution.
- *Restorative Circles:* Use restorative circles to bring members together, discuss issues, and find mutually agreeable solutions. This approach focuses on healing and restoring relationships.

- *Consensus Workshops:* Hold workshops to address conflicts and work towards consensus on contentious issues. These workshops provide a structured environment for discussing and resolving conflicts.

▪ *Examples from Real-World Applications*

- *The Mondragon Corporation:* This is a federation of worker cooperatives in Spain that operates on principles of democratic decision-making and shared ownership. Decisions are made through consensus and voting, ensuring that all members have a voice. Mondragon has successfully navigated economic crises by maintaining a strong sense of solidarity and mutual support.
- *The Pirate Party:* This is a political party that uses liquid democracy, allowing members to delegate their votes to others on specific issues. This flexible approach to decision-making empowers members while maintaining accountability.

▪ *Real-world Applications and Personal Anecdotes*

- *The Mondragon Corporation*: The Mondragon Corporation is a federation of worker cooperatives based in the Basque region of Spain. Founded in 1956 by *Father José María Arizmendiarrieta*, Mondragon has grown to become one of the largest cooperative organizations in the world. It operates on principles of democratic decision-making and shared ownership, with each worker-member having an equal vote in major decisions. Mondragon's success is attributed to its strong commitment to these principles and its ability to adapt to changing economic conditions.

Mondragon's structure includes various cooperatives across different sectors, such as finance, industry, retail, and knowledge. The organization has managed to retain jobs and maintain stability even during economic downturns by fostering a culture of solidarity. Members are willing to accept salary cuts, invest additional funds, and transfer between cooperatives when necessary. This ethos of mutual support has been key to Mondragon's resilience and success.

- *Personal Anecdote:* Imagine a group of neighbors coming together to create a community garden. Instead of appointing a leader, they decide to share responsibilities equally. Each neighbor takes on a task that aligns with their strengths, such as planting, watering, or organizing events. They hold regular meetings to discuss progress and make decisions together. Despite initial challenges, they find that this collaborative approach leads to a more vibrant and successful garden.
- *Humorous Story:* Picture a group of colleagues planning a team-building retreat. Without a designated leader, they initially struggle to agree on the activities. One person suggests a hiking trip, another wants a cooking class, and another proposes a karaoke night. After much debate (and laughter), they decide to combine all three activities into a unique and memorable retreat. This humorous scenario highlights the creative potential of leaderless collaboration.

- *Scriptural Reference*

"For where two or three gather in my name, there am I with them." (Matthew 18:20, NIV). This scripture underscores the power of collective action and the presence of a guiding spirit in group endeavors, resonating with the principles of leaderless leadership.

- *Elaborate Example of Conflict Resolution within a Decentralized Group*

➢ *Case Study: Decentralized Autonomous Organizations (DAOs)*

Decentralized Autonomous Organizations (DAOs) are a modern example of leaderless organizations that operate on blockchain technology. DAOs use smart contracts to automate decision-making processes and governance. However, disputes can still arise, requiring effective conflict resolution mechanisms.

- Conflict Scenario: A DAO focused on funding community projects faces a dispute over the allocation of funds. Some members believe that a particular project should receive more funding, while others disagree, citing concerns about its feasibility and impact.

- *Resolution Process*
- *Initial Discussion:* The dispute is brought to the attention of the entire DAO through a dedicated communication channel. Members are encouraged to share their perspectives and concerns openly.
- *Mediation:* A neutral mediator is appointed to facilitate the discussion. The mediator ensures that all voices are heard and guides the group towards a constructive dialogue.
- *Restorative Circle:* A restorative circle is organized where members discuss the impact of the dispute on the community and explore ways to address the underlying issues. This process helps to rebuild trust and foster a sense of unity.
- *Consensus Workshop:* A workshop is held to work towards a consensus on the funding allocation. Members use techniques like dot voting and the Delphi method to gather input and gradually converge on a decision.
- Final Decision: The agreed-upon decision is implemented through a smart contract, ensuring transparency and accountability.

By following these steps, the DAO successfully resolves the conflict and strengthens its collaborative spirit. This example illustrates how decentralized groups can navigate disputes and maintain harmony without a central authority.

By understanding the mechanics of building a leaderless organization and effective decision-making processes, we can appreciate the potential of this model to transform organizations and movements. Let's continue exploring the ethical considerations and real-world applications of leaderless leadership in the next sections.

Part 3:

Ethical Considerations in Leaderless Leadership

"Ethics is knowing the difference between what you have a right to do and what is right to do."

— Potter Stewart

CHAPTER 5:

Inclusivity and Equal Participation

- *Democratic Decision-Making*

In leaderless organizations, democratic decision-making is paramount. This approach ensures that every member has an equal opportunity to participate in the decision-making process. It fosters a sense of ownership and responsibility among members, as they feel their voices are heard and valued. According to a study by *Harvard Business Review*, ethical leadership involves creating value for society by ensuring inclusivity and participation. This principle aligns with the core values of leaderless leadership, where decisions are made collectively rather than by a single authority. For instance, in the Occupy Wall Street movement, decisions were made through general assemblies where everyone had a voice, demonstrating the power of democratic decision-making.

- *Respect for Diversity*

Respecting diversity is crucial in leaderless organizations. Embracing different perspectives and backgrounds enriches the decision-making process and fosters innovation. Ethical leadership requires valuing others' skills and contributions, promoting mutual respect and healthy workplace relationships. In a leaderless environment, this respect for diversity ensures that all members feel included and valued, leading to a more cohesive and effective organization. For example, the Linux open-source community thrives on contributions from developers worldwide, each bringing unique skills and perspectives.

- *Personal Anecdote*

Imagine a community group working on a local project. Instead of appointing a leader, they decide to operate democratically. Each member, regardless of their background or experience, has an equal say in the decisions. This inclusivity leads to a richer, more innovative project as diverse perspectives are considered and integrated. One member, initially hesitant to speak up, suggests a novel approach that becomes the project's cornerstone, highlighting the value of inclusivity.

- *Scriptural Reference*

"There is neither Jew nor Gentile, neither slave nor free, nor is there male and female, for you are all one in Christ Jesus." (Galatians 3:28, NIV). This scripture emphasizes the importance of inclusivity and equality, resonating with the principles of leaderless leadership.

CHAPTER 6:
Transparency and Accountability

- *Open Communication*

Transparency is a cornerstone of ethical leadership. Open communication ensures that all members are informed and can participate meaningfully in the organization's activities. Ethical leaders encourage their teams to model transparency, fostering a culture of trust and collaboration. In leaderless organizations, transparency helps prevent misunderstandings and promotes accountability, as all actions and decisions are visible to the group. For example, in the Mondragon Corporation, financial information and strategic decisions are openly shared with all members, fostering a sense of trust and collective responsibility.

- *Shared Responsibility*

In leaderless organizations, accountability is distributed among all members. This shared responsibility ensures that everyone is held accountable for their actions and contributions. According to SpringerLink, the ethical imperative in leaderless organizations is that no one should be denied the opportunity to participate in decision-making, and each person has an equal obligation to listen. This principle of shared responsibility helps maintain ethical standards and ensures that the organization functions effectively. For instance, in the *Zapatista movement*, community members collectively manage resources and responsibilities, ensuring accountability and mutual support.

- *Personal Anecdote*

Consider a start-up where all employees share responsibility for the company's success. Without a central leader, they rely on open communication and transparency to coordinate their efforts. This shared responsibility fosters a strong sense of accountability and commitment among the team, driving the start-up's success. When a critical issue arises, the team collaborates to find a solution, demonstrating the power of shared responsibility.

- *Example of How Transparency Impacts Decision-Making*

Transparency significantly impacts decision-making by fostering trust and ensuring that all members are informed. According to Forbes, transparency in the workplace leads to higher employee engagement, better collaboration, and increased trust. For example, in a leaderless tech start-up, transparency about financial health and strategic goals allows all team members to make informed decisions. When the company faces a financial challenge, transparent communication ensures that everyone understands the situation and can contribute to finding a solution. This collective approach not only resolves the issue but also strengthens the team's cohesion and trust.

- *Scriptural Reference*

"The integrity of the upright guides them, but the unfaithful are destroyed by their duplicity." (Proverbs 11:3, NIV). This scripture highlights the importance of integrity and transparency in guiding ethical behavior.

CHAPTER 7:
Ethical Decision-Making

- *Consensus Building*

Consensus-building is essential for ethical decision-making in leaderless organizations. This process ensures that decisions reflect the collective will and ethical standards of the group. Ethical leaders focus on creating value for society by engaging in deliberative decision-making processes. In leaderless organizations, consensus building helps align decisions with the group's values and ethical principles. For instance, the Pirate Party uses liquid democracy, allowing members to delegate their votes on specific issues, ensuring that decisions are made collectively and ethically.

- *Conflict Resolution*

Effective conflict resolution is crucial for maintaining ethical standards in leaderless organizations. Ethical leaders use mediation and restorative practices to address conflicts and rebuild trust. In leaderless environments, conflict resolution mechanisms must be transparent and inclusive, ensuring all voices are heard and respected. For example, in the Mondragon Corporation, conflicts are resolved through mediation and restorative circles, focusing on healing and restoring relationships.

- *Elaborate Example of Conflict Resolution within a Decentralized Group*

➢ *Case Study: The Mondragon Corporation*

The Mondragon Corporation, a federation of worker cooperatives in Spain, provides an excellent example of conflict resolution in a decentralized organization. When conflicts arise, Mondragon uses a structured process to address and resolve issues. This process includes:

- *Initial Discussion:* Conflicts are brought to the attention of the cooperative's members through open communication channels. Members are encouraged to share their perspectives and concerns.
- *Mediation:* Neutral mediators are appointed to facilitate discussions and help resolve conflicts. Mediators ensure that all voices are heard and guide the group towards a resolution.
- *Restorative Circles:* Restorative circles are used to bring members together, discuss the impact of the conflict, and find mutually agreeable solutions. This approach focuses on healing and restoring relationships.
- *Consensus Workshops*: Workshops are held to work towards consensus on contentious issues. Members use techniques like dot voting and the Delphi method to gather input and gradually converge on a decision.
- *Final Decision:* The agreed-upon decision is implemented, ensuring transparency and accountability.

By following these steps, Mondragon successfully resolves conflicts and maintains a strong sense of solidarity and mutual support.

- *Personal Anecdote*

Imagine a volunteer group organizing a community event. A disagreement arises over the event's theme. Instead of letting the conflict escalate, the group holds a restorative circle to discuss the issue. Through open dialogue and mutual respect, they reach a consensus and choose a theme that incorporates everyone's ideas. This process not only resolves the conflict but also strengthens the group's cohesion.

- *Scriptural Reference*

"Blessed are the peacemakers, for they will be called children of God." (Matthew 5:9, NIV). This scripture emphasizes the importance of resolving conflicts peacefully and fostering harmony within the group.

CHAPTER 8:
Empowerment and Trust

- *Empowering Members*

Empowerment is a key aspect of ethical leadership. Ethical leaders encourage their team members to take the initiative and contribute their skills and knowledge. In leaderless organizations, empowerment ensures that all members feel valued and capable of making meaningful contributions. This empowerment fosters a sense of ownership and responsibility, driving the organization's success. For example, in the Linux open-source community, developers are empowered to contribute code and improvements, leading to a robust and innovative software platform.

- *Building Trust*

Trust is the foundation of effective leaderless leadership. Ethical leaders build trust by maintaining transparency, promoting open communication, and demonstrating integrity. In leaderless organizations, trust is essential for collaboration and mutual support. Building trust requires a commitment to ethical principles and a willingness to listen and respect others. For instance, in the Zapatista movement, trust is built through collective decision-making and shared responsibilities, ensuring all members feel valued and respected.

- *Personal Anecdotes*
- Consider a non-profit organization where volunteers are empowered to take on leadership roles. Without a central leader, they rely on trust and mutual respect to coordinate their efforts. This empowerment and trust lead to a more dynamic and effective organization as volunteers feel valued and motivated to contribute their best. When a new volunteer joins, they are

quickly integrated into the team and given meaningful tasks, demonstrating the organization's commitment to empowerment and trust.

- Imagine a tech start-up where employees are encouraged to take ownership of projects. Without a traditional hierarchy, team members trust each other to make decisions and take initiative. One employee, inspired by this trust, develops a new feature that significantly improves the product. This empowerment and trust not only lead to innovation but also strengthen the team's cohesion and morale.

- *Scriptural Reference*

"Trust in the Lord with all your heart and lean not on your own understanding; in all your ways submit to him, and he will make your paths straight." (Proverbs 3:5-6, NIV). This scripture highlights the importance of trust and reliance on ethical principles in guiding actions and decisions.

CHAPTER 9:
Sustainability and Long-Term Vision

- *Ethical Sustainability*

Ethical sustainability involves considering the long-term impact of the organization's actions on the community and environment. Ethical leaders prioritize sustainability by making decisions that balance economic, social, and environmental considerations. In leaderless organizations, sustainability is a collective responsibility, ensuring that the group's actions align with ethical principles and long-term goals. For example, the Mondragon Corporation integrates sustainability into its operations by promoting eco-friendly practices and supporting local communities.

Mondragon's commitment to sustainability is evident in its various initiatives. The corporation invests in renewable energy projects, reduces waste through recycling programs, and supports local agriculture by sourcing materials from nearby farms. These efforts not only benefit the environment but also strengthen the local economy and foster a sense of community.

- *Vision and Values*

A clear vision and set of values are essential for guiding ethical decision-making in leaderless organizations. Ethical leaders articulate a vision that reflects the group's values and inspires members to work towards common goals. In leaderless environments, this vision and set of values provide a framework for decision-making and help maintain ethical standards. For instance, the Zapatista movement's vision of autonomy and social justice guides its actions and decisions, ensuring they align with the community's values.

The Zapatistas emphasize principles such as dignity, democracy, and justice. These values are reflected in their governance structures, prioritizing community participation and collective decision-making. By adhering to these values, the Zapatistas ensure that their actions are consistent with their ethical commitments and long-term vision.

- *Personal Anecdote*

Imagine a cooperative that prioritizes sustainability in its operations. Members collectively decide to implement eco-friendly practices, such as reducing waste and using renewable energy. This commitment to sustainability not only benefits the environment but also strengthens the cooperative's reputation and long-term success. When a new project is proposed, members evaluate its environmental impact and make decisions that align with their sustainability goals. This collective approach ensures the cooperative remains true to its values and vision.

- *Scriptural Reference*

"The earth is the Lord's, and everything in it, the world, and all who live in it." (Psalm 24:1, NIV). This scripture underscores the importance of stewardship and caring for the environment, aligning with the principles of ethical sustainability.

- *Example of Ethical Sustainability in Practice*

➢ *Case Study: Patagonia*

Patagonia, an outdoor clothing company, is renowned for its commitment to sustainability and ethical practices. The company operates on principles of environmental stewardship and social responsibility. Patagonia's mission statement, "We're in business to save our home planet," reflects its dedication to sustainability.

Patagonia implements various sustainable practices, such as using recycled materials, promoting fair labor practices, and donating a portion of its profits to environmental causes. The company also encourages customers to repair and reuse their products rather than buying new ones, reducing waste and promoting a culture of sustainability.

By integrating sustainability into its core values and operations, Patagonia demonstrates how ethical sustainability can drive business success and positively impact the environment and society.

- *Conclusion*

By understanding and addressing the ethical considerations of leaderless leadership, we can create more inclusive, transparent, and sustainable organizations. Ethical sustainability, inclusivity, transparency, accountability, empowerment, and trust are all essential components of effective leaderless leadership. These principles not only guide decision-making but also ensure that the organization remains true to its values and long-term vision.

As we continue exploring the real-world applications and future trends of leaderless leadership in the next sections, we will see how these principles can transform organizations and movements, creating a more equitable and sustainable world.

Part 4:

Mitigating Ethical Dilemmas

"In any moment of decision, the best thing you can do is the right thing, the next best thing is the wrong thing, and the worst thing you can do is nothing."

— Theodore Roosevelt

CHAPTER 10: Decision-Making Authority

- *Establishing Clear Protocols*

In leaderless organizations, the absence of a central authority can lead to confusion and inefficiency if clear decision-making protocols are not established. To mitigate this, it is essential to develop structured processes that outline how decisions are made, who is involved, and how disagreements are handled. These protocols should be transparent and inclusive, ensuring all members understand and agree to the decision-making framework.

For example, the Mondragon Corporation uses a democratic voting system where major decisions are made through a majority vote of its members. This system ensures that all voices are heard and that decisions reflect the collective will of the group. Additionally, the Linux open-source community employs a similar approach, where contributors vote on key changes and updates to the software, ensuring that decisions are made collaboratively.

- *Rotating Leadership Roles*

Another effective strategy is to implement rotating leadership roles for specific tasks or projects. This approach distributes leadership responsibilities among members, preventing the concentration of power and encouraging diverse perspectives. Rotating roles also provide opportunities for members to develop leadership skills and gain experience in different areas.

For instance, in the Linux open-source community, project maintainers often rotate, allowing different contributors to take on leadership roles and bring fresh ideas to the project. This rotation not only prevents burnout but also fosters a culture of continuous learning and innovation.

- *Personal Anecdote*

Imagine a community theater group where leadership roles rotate for each production. One member directs the first play, another handles the next, and so on. This rotation ensures that everyone has a chance to lead and contribute their unique vision, resulting in a diverse and dynamic repertoire of performances.

- *Scriptural Reference*

"For just as each of us has one body with many members, and these members do not all have the same function, so in Christ we, though many, form one body, and each member belongs to all the others." (Romans 12:4-5, NIV). This scripture highlights the importance of diverse roles and shared responsibilities within a community.

CHAPTER 11:
Accountability and Responsibility

- *Defining Roles and Responsibilities*

Clearly defining the roles and responsibilities of each member is crucial for ensuring accountability in leaderless organizations. This clarity helps prevent overlap and confusion, ensuring that everyone knows what is expected of them. Detailed role descriptions and regular reviews can help maintain accountability and ensure that tasks are completed efficiently.

For example, in the Zapatista movement, community members have clearly defined roles and responsibilities, which are regularly reviewed and adjusted as needed. This structure ensures that everyone contributes to the community's goals and that accountability is maintained.

- *Regular Check-Ins*

Regular check-ins and progress reviews are essential for maintaining accountability and addressing any issues promptly. These check-ins provide opportunities for members to discuss their progress, share challenges, and seek support from the group. They also help ensure that everyone stays aligned with the organization's goals and values.

For instance, in the Mondragon Corporation, regular meetings are held to review progress and address any issues. These meetings foster a culture of transparency and accountability, ensuring that all members are engaged and informed.

- *Personal Anecdote*

Consider a start-up where employees hold weekly check-ins to discuss their progress and challenges. These meetings provide a platform for open communication and mutual support, ensuring everyone stays on track and feels accountable for their contributions.

- *Scriptural Reference*

"Therefore encourage one another and build each other up, just as in fact you are doing." (1 Thessalonians 5:11, NIV). This scripture emphasizes the importance of regular encouragement and support within a community.

CHAPTER 12:
Conflict Resolution

- *Conflict Resolution Mechanisms*

Effective conflict resolution mechanisms are essential for maintaining harmony and ethical standards in leaderless organizations. These mechanisms should be transparent, inclusive, and focused on finding mutually agreeable solutions. Mediation, restorative circles, and consensus workshops are some effective strategies for resolving conflicts.

For example, the Mondragon Corporation uses mediation and restorative circles to address conflicts. These approaches focus on healing and restoring relationships, ensuring all voices are heard and respected.

- *Training in Conflict Management*

Providing training in conflict management and resolution techniques can help members navigate conflicts more effectively. This training equips members with the skills and tools needed to address disputes constructively and maintain a positive and collaborative environment.

For instance, in the Zapatista movement, members receive training in conflict resolution and mediation, ensuring they can handle disputes effectively and maintain community cohesion.

- *Personal Anecdote*

Imagine a volunteer group organizing a community event. A disagreement arises over the event's theme. Instead of letting the conflict escalate, the group holds a restorative circle to discuss the issue. Through open dialogue and mutual respect, they reach a consensus and choose a theme that incorporates everyone's ideas. This process not only resolves the conflict but also strengthens the group's cohesion.

- *Additional Example of Conflict Resolution*

➢ *Case Study: The Pirate Party*

The Pirate Party, a political organization that advocates for digital rights and transparency, often faces conflicts due to its decentralized structure. To resolve these conflicts, the party uses a combination of online forums and face-to-face meetings where members can discuss issues openly. They also employ liquid democracy, allowing members to delegate their votes to others on specific issues, ensuring that decisions are made collectively and ethically.

- *Scriptural Reference*

"Blessed are the peacemakers, for they will be called children of God." (Matthew 5:9, NIV). This scripture emphasizes the importance of resolving conflicts peacefully and fostering harmony within the group.

CHAPTER 13: Ethical Standards and Consistency

- *Developing a Code of Ethics*

A comprehensive code of ethics is essential for guiding behavior and decision-making in leaderless organizations. This code should outline the expected behavior and ethical standards for all members, providing a clear framework for maintaining integrity and accountability.

For example, the Mondragon Corporation has a code of ethics that emphasizes principles such as solidarity, participation, and social responsibility. This code guides the behavior of its members and ensures that the organization operates ethically and consistently.

- *Ethics Committees*

Forming ethics committees can help oversee adherence to ethical standards and address any ethical concerns. These committees can provide guidance, review ethical issues, and ensure that the organization's actions align with its values and principles.

For instance, in the Linux open-source community, ethics committees review contributions and ensure they adhere to the community's standards and values.

- *Personal Anecdote*

Consider a cooperative where members develop a code of ethics that emphasizes sustainability and social responsibility. An ethics committee is formed to oversee adherence to this code, ensuring that all actions and decisions align with the cooperative's values. This structure helps maintain ethical standards and fosters a culture of integrity.

- *Scriptural Reference*

"The integrity of the upright guides them, but the unfaithful are destroyed by their duplicity." (Proverbs 11:3, NIV). This scripture highlights the importance of integrity and ethical behavior in guiding actions and decisions.

CHAPTER 14:
Resource Allocation

▪ *Transparent Allocation Processes*

Implementing transparent processes for resource allocation is crucial for ensuring fairness and preventing disputes. These processes should be clear, inclusive, and based on agreed-upon criteria. Transparency in resource allocation helps build trust and ensures that all members understand how and why resources are distributed.

For example, in the Mondragon Corporation, resource allocation decisions are made through democratic processes, ensuring that all members have a say in how resources are distributed.

▪ *Participatory Budgeting*

Participatory budgeting is an effective approach for involving members in resource allocation decisions. This process allows members to propose and vote on budget allocations, ensuring that resources are distributed according to the group's priorities and needs.

For instance, in the Zapatista movement, participatory budgeting is used to allocate resources for community projects. This approach ensures that resources are distributed fairly and transparently, reflecting the community's collective priorities.

▪ *Resource Allocation Challenges*

Resource allocation in leaderless organizations can present several challenges:

- *Overallocation and Underutilization:* Balancing workloads can be difficult without a central authority. Overallocated resources can lead to burnout, while underutilized resources result in inefficiencies.

- *Skill Gaps:* Identifying and addressing skill gaps within the organization can be challenging, especially as needs evolve.
- *Communication Issues:* Ensuring that all members are informed about resource allocation decisions can be difficult, leading to misunderstandings and conflicts.

- *Personal Anecdote*

Imagine a community organization that uses participatory budgeting to allocate funds for local projects. Members propose and vote on different projects, ensuring that resources are distributed according to the community's needs and priorities. This process fosters a sense of ownership and accountability, as members feel directly involved in decision-making.

- *Scriptural Reference*

"Each of you should give what you have decided in your heart to give, not reluctantly or under compulsion, for God loves a cheerful giver." (2 Corinthians 9:7, NIV). This scripture emphasizes the importance of giving and resource allocation based on collective decision-making and generosity.

CHAPTER 15:

Transparency and Trust

- *Open Communication Channels*

Maintaining open and transparent communication channels is essential for building trust and ensuring all members are informed and engaged. These channels should facilitate open dialogue, information sharing, and collaboration, helping to prevent misunderstandings and promote accountability.

For example, in the Mondragon Corporation, open communication channels are maintained through regular meetings, newsletters, and digital platforms. These channels ensure that all members are informed and can participate meaningfully in the organization's activities. Similarly, the Linux open-source community uses mailing lists, forums, and collaborative platforms like GitHub to keep contributors informed and engaged.

- *Trust-Building Activities*

Engaging in regular trust-building activities and exercises can help strengthen relationships and foster a culture of trust. These activities can include team-building exercises, collaborative projects, and social events, helping to build rapport and mutual respect among members.

For instance, in the Linux open-source community, hackathons and collaborative coding sessions are used to build trust and foster collaboration among developers. These events provide opportunities for contributors to work together, share knowledge, and build relationships.

- *Personal Anecdote*

Consider a non-profit organization that holds regular team-building activities to strengthen trust among volunteers. These activities include collaborative projects, social events, and workshops, helping to build rapport and mutual respect. As a result, volunteers feel more connected and motivated to contribute their best efforts.

- *Scriptural Reference*

"Trust in the Lord with all your heart and lean not on your own understanding; in all your ways submit to him, and he will make your paths straight." (Proverbs 3:5-6, NIV). This scripture highlights the importance of trust and reliance on ethical principles in guiding actions and decisions.

CHAPTER 16:
Additional Strategies

- *Regular Ethical Audits*

Conducting regular ethical audits can help assess the organization's adherence to ethical standards and identify areas for improvement. These audits should be transparent and involve input from all members, ensuring that the organization's actions align with its values and principles.

For example, the Mondragon Corporation conducts regular ethical audits to review its practices and ensure they align with its code of ethics. These audits involve evaluating financial practices, environmental impact, and social responsibility, ensuring the organization maintains high ethical standards.

- *Feedback Mechanisms*

Establishing robust feedback mechanisms allows members to voice their concerns and suggestions anonymously if needed. This feedback helps identify potential ethical issues and areas for improvement, fostering a culture of continuous learning and adaptation.

For instance, in the Zapatista movement, feedback mechanisms are used to gather input from community members on various issues. This feedback is then used to make informed decisions and address any concerns, ensuring that the community remains responsive and adaptive.

- *Continuous Learning*

Promoting a culture of continuous learning and improvement is essential for maintaining ethical standards in leaderless organizations. This involves providing ongoing training and development opportunities for members, ensuring they stay informed about best practices in ethical leadership.

For example, the Linux open-source community encourages continuous learning through workshops, webinars, and collaborative projects. These opportunities help contributors stay updated on the latest developments and best practices in software development and ethical leadership.

- *Personal Anecdote*

Imagine a cooperative that conducts regular ethical audits and encourages continuous learning among its members. The cooperative holds workshops on ethical practices, sustainability, and social responsibility, ensuring all members are informed and engaged. This commitment to continuous learning helps the cooperative maintain high ethical standards and adapt to changing circumstances.

- *Scriptural Reference*

"Let the wise listen and add to their learning, and let the discerning get guidance." (Proverbs 1:5, NIV). This scripture emphasizes the importance of continuous learning and seeking guidance to maintain ethical standards.

- *Conclusion*

By understanding and addressing the ethical considerations of leaderless leadership, we can create more inclusive, transparent, and sustainable organizations. Ethical sustainability, inclusivity, transparency, accountability, empowerment, and trust are all essential components of effective leaderless leadership. These principles not only guide decision-making but also ensure that the organization remains true to its values and long-term vision.

As we continue exploring the real-world applications and future trends of leaderless leadership in the next sections, we will see how these principles can transform organizations and movements, creating a more equitable and sustainable world.

Part 5:

Leaderless Leadership in Action

"The function of leadership is to produce more leaders, not more followers."

— Ralph Nader

CHAPTER 17:
Case Studies

- *Detailed Analysis of Leaderless Organizations and Movements*

➢ *Occupy Wall Street*

Occupy Wall Street (OWS) began in 2011 as a protest against economic inequality and corporate influence on government. The movement was notable for its leaderless structure, relying on general assemblies and consensus-based decision-making. Participants used hand signals to express agreement or disagreement, ensuring everyone had a voice. Despite lacking a central leadership figure, OWS managed to organize large-scale protests and gain significant media attention.

- *Key Takeaways*

✓ *Inclusivity:* OWS's leaderless structure allowed for diverse voices and perspectives, fostering a sense of inclusivity.

✓ *Innovation:* The use of hand signals and consensus-based decision-making were innovative approaches to managing large groups without a central leader.

✓ *Challenges:* The lack of a clear leadership structure sometimes led to inefficiencies and difficulties in coordinating actions.

➢ *The Arab Spring*

The Arab Spring was a series of anti-government protests and uprisings across the Arab world in the early 2010s. These movements were largely leaderless, relying on social media and grassroots organizing to mobilize people. The lack of a central authority made it difficult for regimes to suppress the movements, highlighting the power of collective action.

- *Key Takeaways*
  - ✓ *Empowerment: Social media empowered individuals to organize and mobilize without a central leader.*
  - ✓ *Resilience:* The decentralized nature of the movements made them more resilient to suppression.
  - ✓ *Challenges:* Coordination and sustaining momentum were challenging without a central leadership figure.

➢ *The Linux Open Source Project*

The Linux operating system is developed through a collaborative effort by programmers around the world. The project operates without a central authority, with contributors working together to improve the software. Decisions are made through consensus and meritocracy, where the best ideas rise to the top.

- *Key Takeaways*
  - ✓ *Collaboration:* The open-source model fosters collaboration and innovation by allowing anyone to contribute.
  - ✓ *Transparency:* All contributions and decisions are made transparently, ensuring accountability.
  - ✓ *Challenges:* Coordinating contributions from a global community can be complex and requires robust communication tools.

▪ *Personal Anecdote*

Imagine a group of students working on a group project. Instead of appointing a leader, they decide to share responsibilities equally. Each student takes on a task that aligns with their strengths, and they regularly meet to discuss progress and make decisions together. Despite initial challenges, they find that this collaborative approach leads to a more innovative and well-rounded project.

- *Humorous Story*

Picture a group of friends planning a surprise party. Without a designated leader, they initially struggle to agree on the theme. One person suggests a beach party, another wants a superhero theme, and another proposes a masquerade ball. After much debate (and laughter), they decide to combine all three themes into a unique and unforgettable party. This humorous scenario highlights the creative potential of leaderless collaboration.

- *Scriptural Reference*

"As iron sharpens iron, so one person sharpens another." (Proverbs 27:17, NIV). This scripture emphasizes the importance of mutual support and collaboration, which are essential components of leaderless leadership.

CHAPTER 18:

Leaderless Leadership in Different Sectors

- *Business and Start-ups*

Leaderless leadership can be particularly effective in business and start-up environments, where innovation and agility are crucial. Companies like Valve Corporation, a video game developer, operate with a flat organizational structure where employees have the freedom to choose their projects and collaborate without a central authority.

- *Key Takeaways*

✓ *Innovation:* Flat structures encourage creativity and innovation by allowing employees to pursue their passions.

✓ *Flexibility:* Without rigid hierarchies, companies can adapt quickly to changing market conditions.

✓ *Challenges:* Ensuring accountability and coordinating efforts can be challenging without a clear leadership structure.

- *Social Movements and Activism*

Leaderless leadership is also effective in social movements and activism, where grassroots organizing and collective action are essential. The Black Lives Matter (BLM) movement, for example, operates with a decentralized structure, allowing local chapters to organize independently while adhering to shared principles and goals.

- *Key Takeaways*
  - ✓ *Empowerment:* Decentralized structures empower local chapters to take action and address specific community needs.
  - ✓ *Resilience:* The movement's decentralized nature makes it more resilient to external pressures and suppression.
  - ✓ *Challenges:* Maintaining cohesion and consistency across different chapters can be difficult without a central leadership figure.

- *Technology and Innovation*

In the technology sector, leaderless leadership can drive innovation by fostering collaboration and open-source development. Projects like Wikipedia and the Apache Software Foundation rely on contributions from a global community of volunteers operating without a central authority.

- *Key Takeaways*
  - ✓ *Collaboration:* Open-source projects thrive on collaboration and collective problem-solving.
  - ✓ *Transparency:* Transparent processes ensure accountability and trust within the community.
  - ✓ *Challenges:* Coordinating contributions and maintaining quality control can be complex in a decentralized environment.

- *Personal Anecdote*

Consider a tech start-up where employees are encouraged to take ownership of projects. Without a traditional hierarchy, team members trust each other to make decisions and take initiative. One employee, inspired by this trust, develops a new feature that significantly improves the product. This empowerment and trust not only lead to innovation but also strengthen the team's cohesion and morale.

- *Scriptural Reference*

"For just as each of us has one body with many members, and these members do not all have the same function, so in Christ we, though many, form one body, and each member belongs to all the others." (Romans 12:4-5, NIV). This scripture highlights the importance of diverse roles and shared responsibilities within a community.

- *Conclusion*

By examining these case studies and exploring the application of leaderless leadership in different sectors, we can see the transformative potential of this model. Leaderless leadership fosters inclusivity, innovation, and resilience, making it a powerful approach for organizations and movements seeking to create positive change. As we continue to explore the future trends and impact of leaderless leadership in the next sections, we will uncover how this model can shape a more equitable and sustainable world.

Part 6:

The Future of Leaderless Leadership

"The future belongs to those who believe in the beauty of their dreams."

— Eleanor Roosevelt

CHAPTER 19:
The Impact of Technology

- *How AI and Blockchain Are Shaping Leaderless Leadership*

Artificial Intelligence (AI) and blockchain technology are revolutionizing how leaderless organizations operate. AI can enhance decision-making processes by providing data-driven insights and automating routine tasks, allowing members to focus on strategic initiatives. For example, AI can analyze large datasets to identify trends and predict outcomes, helping organizations make informed decisions quickly. Blockchain, with its decentralized and transparent nature, ensures that all transactions and decisions are recorded immutably, fostering trust and accountability. This technology can be used to create smart contracts that automatically execute agreements when predefined conditions are met, reducing the need for intermediaries and enhancing efficiency.

For example, Decentralized Autonomous Organizations (DAOs) leverage blockchain technology to operate without a central authority. Smart contracts automate governance and decision-making processes, ensuring transparency and reducing the risk of fraud. AI can further enhance these processes by analyzing data to predict trends and optimize resource allocation. By integrating AI and blockchain, leaderless organizations can achieve higher levels of efficiency, transparency, and trust.

- *Key Takeaways*

✓ *Efficiency:* AI automates routine tasks, freeing up members to focus on strategic initiatives.

✓ *Transparency:* Blockchain ensures that all transactions and decisions are recorded immutably, fostering trust.

✓ *Challenges:* Integrating these technologies requires technical expertise and can be costly.

- *Scriptural Reference*

"For lack of guidance a nation falls, but victory is won through many advisers." (Proverbs 11:14, NIV). This scripture highlights the importance of collective wisdom and guidance, which can be enhanced through technology in leaderless organizations.

CHAPTER 20:
The Role of Social Media and Digital Platforms

- *The Power of Social Media in Leaderless Movements*

Social media platforms have become powerful tools for organizing and mobilizing leaderless movements. They enable rapid communication, coordination, and dissemination of information, allowing movements to gain momentum quickly. Platforms like Tick Tock, Twitter (X spaces), Facebook, and Instagram have been instrumental in movements such as the Arab Spring and Black Lives Matter. These platforms allow activists to share real-time updates, organize events, and amplify their messages to a global audience.

Social media also democratizes information dissemination, giving a voice to marginalized groups and enabling grassroots movements to challenge established power structures. However, the reliance on social media also presents challenges, such as the spread of misinformation and the need for digital literacy to navigate these platforms effectively.

- *Key Takeaways*

✓ *Mobilization:* Social media enables rapid mobilization and coordination of efforts.

✓ *Visibility:* These platforms provide visibility and amplify the voices of marginalized groups.

✓ *Challenges:* The spread of misinformation and the need for digital literacy are significant challenges.

- *Personal Anecdote*

Imagine a grassroots environmental movement that uses social media to organize clean-up events. Without a central leader, volunteers coordinate through a Facebook group, sharing updates and organizing logistics. This decentralized approach allows the movement to grow organically and engage a wider audience.

- *Scriptural Reference*

"Let us not give up meeting together, as some are in the habit of doing, but encouraging one another – and all the more as you see the Day approaching." (Hebrews 10:25, NIV). This scripture emphasizes the importance of coming together and supporting one another, which social media facilitates in leaderless movements.

CHAPTER 21:
Future Trends and Predictions

Emerging Trends in Leaderless Leadership

- *Increased Digitization*

The future of leaderless leadership will be heavily influenced by increased digitization. Organizations will leverage technologies such as the Internet of Things (IoTs), machine learning (ML), and cloud computing, just to mention but a few, to enhance collaboration and efficiency. These technologies will enable real-time data sharing and decision-making, making leaderless organizations more agile and responsive. For instance, IoT devices can provide real-time data on operational performance, while cloud computing allows for seamless collaboration across geographically dispersed teams.

- *Key Takeaways*

✓ *Agility:* Digitization enhances the agility and responsiveness of leaderless organizations.
✓ *Collaboration:* Real-time data sharing fosters collaboration and informed decision-making.
✓ *Challenges:* Ensuring data security and privacy will be critical.

- *Holacracy and Self-Management*

Holacracy and self-management are gaining traction as models for leaderless organizations. These approaches distribute authority and decision-making across the organization, allowing teams to self-organize and operate autonomously. Companies like Zappos have adopted holacracy to foster innovation and employee engagement. In a holacratic organization, roles are defined around work, not people, and authority is distributed to teams rather than centralized in a hierarchy.

- *Key Takeaways*
- ✓ *Empowerment:* Holacracy empowers employees by giving them more control over their work.
- ✓ *Innovation:* Self-management fosters a culture of innovation and continuous improvement.
- ✓ *Challenges:* Implementing these models requires a cultural shift and ongoing support.

- *Focus on Diversity, Equity, and Inclusion (DEI)*

Future leaderless organizations will place a strong emphasis on diversity, equity, and inclusion. By fostering diverse and inclusive environments, these organizations can leverage a wide range of perspectives and experiences, driving innovation and resilience. DEI initiatives will become integral to organizational strategies, ensuring all members feel valued and included.

- *Key Takeaways*
- ✓ *Innovation:* Diverse teams bring a variety of perspectives, fostering innovation.
- ✓ *Resilience:* Inclusive environments are more resilient and adaptable.
- ✓ *Challenges:* Ensuring genuine inclusion and addressing unconscious biases will be ongoing challenges.

- *Scriptural Reference*

"There is neither Jew nor Gentile, neither slave nor free, nor is there male and female, for you are all one in Christ Jesus." (Galatians 3:28, NIV). This scripture underscores the importance of inclusivity and equality, aligning with the principles of DEI in leaderless organizations.

CHAPTER 22:
Preparing for a Leaderless Future

- *Skills and Mindsets Needed*

To thrive in leaderless organizations, individuals need to develop specific skills and mindsets. These include adaptability, collaboration, and a commitment to continuous learning. Leaders in such environments must be comfortable with ambiguity and capable of facilitating rather than directing. Adaptability is crucial as it allows individuals to respond effectively to changing circumstances. Collaboration skills are essential for working in decentralized teams, and a commitment to continuous learning ensures that individuals stay relevant and contribute effectively.

- *Key Takeaways*

✓ *Adaptability:* The ability to adapt to changing circumstances is crucial.

✓ *Collaboration:* Effective collaboration skills are essential for working in decentralized teams.

✓ *Continuous Learning:* A commitment to continuous learning ensures that individuals stay relevant and contribute effectively.

- *Educational and Training Programs*

Educational institutions and organizations will need to develop training programs that equip individuals with the skills needed for leaderless environments. These programs should focus on collaborative leadership, conflict resolution, and digital literacy. For example, universities can offer courses on decentralized management and ethical leadership, while organizations can provide workshops on conflict resolution and team collaboration.

- *Key Takeaways*
- ✓ *Collaborative Leadership:* Training programs should emphasize the importance of collaborative leadership.
- ✓ *Conflict Resolution:* Equipping individuals with conflict resolution skills is essential.
- ✓ *Digital Literacy:* Ensuring digital literacy will be critical for leveraging technology effectively.

- *Policy Implications and Societal Impact*

The rise of leaderless organizations will have significant policy implications and societal impacts. Policymakers will need to consider how to support these organizations through regulations and incentives. Additionally, the shift towards leaderless models may influence broader societal norms around leadership and governance. For example, policies that promote flexible work arrangements and support for digital infrastructure can facilitate the growth of leaderless organizations.

- *Key Takeaways*
- ✓ *Regulatory Support:* Policymakers should consider regulations that support leaderless organizations.
- ✓ *Societal Norms:* The shift towards leaderless models may influence societal norms around leadership.
- ✓ *Challenges:* Balancing innovation with regulation will be a key challenge.

- *Scriptural Reference*

"Plans fail for lack of counsel, but with many advisers they succeed." (Proverbs 15:22, NIV). This scripture highlights the importance of collective wisdom and collaboration, which are essential for the success of leaderless organizations.

- *Conclusion*

The future of leaderless leadership is bright, with technology, social media, and emerging trends shaping the way organizations operate. By embracing these changes and preparing for the challenges ahead, leaderless organizations can create more inclusive, innovative, and resilient environments. As we move forward, the principles of leaderless leadership will continue to transform organizations and societies, fostering a more equitable and sustainable world.

CHAPTER 23:
Real-World Champions of Leaderless Leadership: Lessons from Visionaries

- *Introduction*

In the journey towards leaderless leadership, we find inspiration in the lives of remarkable individuals who have championed inclusivity, transparency, ethical decision-making, empowerment, and sustainability. Their stories not only illustrate these principles but also provide valuable lessons for creating more resilient and innovative organizations.

Malala Yousafzai: The Voice of Inclusivity

Quote:

"One child, one teacher, one book, one pen can change the world."

In Kenya, this sounds like the discussion of *"one man, one Shilling, one vote, one kilometer"*. If you know, you know!

Humor:

Who knew that skipping school could lead to a Nobel Prize?

Scriptural Support:

"Plans fail for lack of counsel, but with many advisers they succeed." (Proverbs 15:22, NIV)

Impact:

Malala's advocacy for girls' education underscores the power of inclusivity and equal participation. Her courage in the face of adversity has inspired global movements for education and women's rights.

Elon Musk: The Transparent Innovator

Quote:

"When something is important enough, you do it even if the odds are not in your favor."

Humor:

Elon's idea of a vacation is launching a car into space. Talk about taking work home!

Scriptural Support:

"For we are taking pains to do what is right, not only in the eyes of the Lord but also in the eyes of man." (2 Corinthians 8:21, NIV)

Impact:

Musk's transparent leadership style and ambitious goals have driven significant advancements in technology and renewable energy, showcasing the importance of transparency and accountability.

Greta Thunberg: The Ethical Crusader

Quote:

"I have learned you are never too small to make a difference."

Humor:

Greta's idea of a school project? Saving the planet.

Scriptural Support:

"The earth is the Lord's, and everything in it, the world, and all who live in it." (Psalm 24:1, NIV)

Impact:
Greta's activism highlights the importance of ethical decision-making and sustainability. Her efforts have mobilized millions to take action against climate change.

Linus Torvalds: The Empowering Technologist
Quote:
"Talk is cheap. Show me the code."

Humor:
Linus's idea of a fun weekend? Debugging the universe.

Scriptural Support:
"Whatever you do, work at it with all your heart, as working for the Lord, not for human masters." (Colossians 3:23, NIV)

Impact:
Torvalds' creation of Linux and the open-source movement exemplifies empowerment and trust. His work has fostered a global community of collaboration and innovation.

Yvon Chouinard: The Sustainable Pioneer
Quote:
"The more you know, the less you need."

Humor:
Yvon's idea of a business meeting? Climbing a mountain.

Scriptural Support:
"The righteous care for the needs of their animals, but the kindest acts of the wicked are cruel." (Proverbs 12:10, NIV)

Impact:
Chouinard's commitment to ethical sustainability at Patagonia demonstrates that businesses can thrive while prioritizing environmental and social responsibility.

Vitalik Buterin: The Decentralized Visionary
Quote:
"Blockchain solves the problem of manipulation. In the digital world, trust is everything."

Humor:
Vitalik's idea of a light read? The Ethereum white paper.

Scriptural Support:
"Let all things be done decently and in order." (1 Corinthians 14:40, NIV)

Impact:
Buterin's work with Ethereum has revolutionized digital contracts and decentralized applications, promoting transparency and democratic decision-making.

Sal Khan: The Educational Innovator
Quote:
"You only have to know one thing: You can learn anything."

Humor:
Sal's idea of a classroom? The entire internet.

Scriptural Support:
"The heart of the discerning acquires knowledge, for the ears of the wise seek it out." (Proverbs 18:15, NIV)

Impact:
Khan's creation of Khan Academy has democratized access to education, providing free resources to millions and emphasizing the importance of continuous learning.

In "The New Era of Leaderless Leadership: Empowering Voices, Inspiring Change," other "characters" are not individuals but rather the collective groups and movements that embody leaderless leadership. These include:

1. *The Occupy Wall Street Protesters:* A diverse group of individuals united by their desire to challenge economic inequality and corporate influence. They exemplify the power of collective action without a central leader.
2. *The #EndSARS Activists:* Driven by a shared goal to end police brutality in Nigeria, these activists used social media to organize and amplify their voices, demonstrating the strength of decentralized leadership.
3. *The GenZ Protesters in Kenya:* Young Kenyans who organized leaderless protests against government opulence and tax hikes, showcasing the impact of digital communication in mobilizing collective action.
4. *The Linux Open Source Community:* Programmers from around the world who collaborate to develop high-quality software without a central authority, highlighting the innovative potential of leaderless leadership.
5. *The Zapatista Movement*: A group in Mexico that emphasizes collective decision-making and community autonomy, challenging traditional power structures and promoting inclusivity.

These "characters" illustrate the diverse applications and profound impact of leaderless leadership in various contexts.

- *Conclusion*

These real-world champions of leaderless leadership illustrate the transformative power of inclusivity, transparency, ethical decision-making, empowerment, and sustainability. Their stories provide a roadmap for organizations and societies seeking to embrace these principles and create a more inclusive, innovative, and resilient future. As we learn from their journeys, we are reminded of the scriptural wisdom that guides us: "Plans fail for lack of counsel, but with many advisers they succeed." (Proverbs 15:22, NIV).

Part 7:

A New Dawn

"You have to act as if it were possible to radically transform the world. And you have to do it all the time."

— Angela Davis

CHAPTER 24:
Leaderless Movements in Modern Politics: A New Paradigm

- *Introduction*

In recent years, the political landscape has witnessed a significant shift towards leaderless movements. These movements, characterized by their decentralized nature and collective leadership, have emerged as powerful forces for change. As the renowned activist and scholar Angela Davis once said, "You have to act as if it were possible to radically transform the world. And you have to do it all the time." This quote underscores the relentless commitment required to drive meaningful change. It emphasizes the importance of continuous, collective effort in challenging the status quo and striving for a better future.

Leaderless movements have demonstrated that change can be driven by the collective strength and shared goals of their participants, rather than relying on a single charismatic leader. This chapter explores the significance of leaderless leadership in modern politics, highlighting its impact on fostering creativity, empowering voices, and inspiring change. By examining historical and contemporary examples, we will delve into the dynamics of these movements, their strengths and weaknesses, and their implications for future leadership.

- *The Rise of Leaderless Movements*
- *Historical Context:* Leaderless movements are not a new phenomenon. Historically, movements such as the Arab Spring demonstrated the power of collective action without a central figurehead. These movements relied on the collective strength and shared goals of their participants to drive change. The Arab Spring, which began in late 2010, saw a series of anti-

government protests, uprisings, and armed rebellions that spread across much of the Arab world. The movement was largely decentralized, with no single leader directing the actions, yet it managed to topple several long-standing regimes.

- *Modern Examples:* In recent years, several leaderless movements have gained prominence. The Hong Kong protests, which began in 2019, were marked by their decentralized organization and lack of a single leader. Protesters used social media and encrypted messaging apps to coordinate actions, demonstrating the effectiveness of collective leadership.

Similarly, the Black Lives Matter movement, which started as a hashtag in 2013, has grown into a global movement advocating for racial justice without a central leadership structure. BLM has brought attention to systemic racism and police brutality, inspiring similar movements worldwide.

- *The Power of Collective Voices*
- *Empowerment:* Leaderless movements empower individuals by providing a platform for diverse voices to be heard. This inclusivity allows for a broader range of perspectives and ideas, fostering a sense of ownership and participation among members. When individuals feel that their voices matter, they are more likely to engage actively and contribute to the movement's goals.

➢ *Case Study: #MeToo Movement*

The #MeToo movement is a prime example of how leaderless movements can bring attention to critical issues. Originating as a social media campaign, #MeToo empowered survivors of sexual harassment and assault to share their stories, leading to widespread awareness and significant societal impact. The movement's decentralized nature allowed for a diverse range of voices to be heard, from high-profile celebrities to everyday individuals. This inclusivity helped to create a powerful collective voice that challenged systemic issues and led to tangible changes in policies and practices across various industries.

- *Challenges and Opportunities*
- *Strengths:* Leaderless movements possess several strengths, including flexibility and adaptability. Without a central leader, these movements can quickly respond to changing circumstances and incorporate diverse viewpoints. This grassroots support often leads to a strong sense of community and solidarity among participants. The decentralized structure allows for a more democratic and inclusive approach, where decisions are made collectively, and everyone's voice can be heard.
- Weaknesses: However, leaderless movements also face challenges. The lack of clear objectives and centralized coordination can lead to disorganization and fragmentation. Without a central figure to unify the movement, it can be difficult to maintain a consistent message and strategy. Additionally, the absence of a single spokesperson can make it challenging to negotiate with authorities or articulate a unified stance. These weaknesses can sometimes hinder the movement's effectiveness and sustainability.

The lack of clear objectives and centralized coordination can lead to disorganization and fragmentation. For example, during the Occupy Wall Street movement, the absence of a unified strategy and clear leadership led to internal conflicts and a lack of direction, ultimately weakening the movement's impact. Similarly, the Arab Spring saw varying degrees of success across different countries, with some movements struggling to maintain cohesion and achieve their goals due to disorganization.

- *Overcoming Challenges*

To overcome these challenges, leaderless movements can adopt several strategies:

1. Establishing Clear Goals: Defining specific, achievable objectives can help maintain focus and direction. Clear goals provide a common purpose that unites participants and guides their actions.
2. Creating Communication Channels: Effective communication is crucial for coordination. Utilizing social media, encrypted messaging apps, and regular meetings can help ensure that participants are informed and aligned.
3. Building Alliances: Forming alliances with other organizations and movements can provide additional resources and support. These partnerships can help amplify the movement's message and increase its impact.
4. Empowering Local Leaders: While maintaining a decentralized structure, empowering local leaders can help manage and coordinate activities at a grassroots level. These leaders can act as points of contact and facilitate communication and organization within their communities.

- *Future Opportunities*

Looking ahead, leaderless movements have the potential to drive significant change in various sectors:

1. Political Reform: By advocating for more inclusive and participatory governance, leaderless movements can influence political systems and promote democratic reforms.
2. Social Justice: These movements can continue to raise awareness and drive action on critical social issues, such as racial justice, gender equality, and environmental sustainability.
3. Technological Innovation: Leveraging technology to organize and mobilize can enhance the effectiveness of

leaderless movements. Innovations in communication tools and platforms can facilitate coordination and amplify their reach.

- *Real-Life Examples*

Kenya:

#OccupyParliament

The #OccupyParliament movement in Kenya emerged in response to the controversial Finance Bill 2024, which proposed significant tax increases. On June 25, 2024, thousands of protesters, primarily from Generation Z, stormed the Kenyan Parliament Building in Nairobi. The decentralized nature of the protest allowed for a massive turnout, with demonstrators using social media to coordinate their actions. The protest resulted in the deaths of some people and injuries to many others. The movement successfully pressured President William Ruto to veto the bill, demonstrating the power of collective action.

#OccupyChurches

The #OccupyChurches movement in Kenya is another powerful example of how faith communities can play a crucial role in social activism. In 2024, Generation Z protesters took their fight against the controversial Finance Bill to the churches, creatively using the hashtag #OccupyChurches. They disrupted church services and fundraisers, demanding an end to political donations to and calling for accountability from religious leaders who they accused of being subservient to the political class. This movement highlighted the potential of religious institutions to act as catalysts for change, reinforcing the idea that collective action can transcend traditional boundaries and unite people from diverse backgrounds.

#OccupyJKIA

In July 2024, young Kenyans threatened to storm Jomo Kenyatta International Airport (JKIA) to protest against the government's policies. The movement, known as #OccupyJKIA, aimed to disrupt air traffic and draw attention to their demands. Although the protest at the airport was thwarted by heavy security, the demonstrators managed to gather in large numbers in Nairobi, catching the police by surprise. This movement highlighted the ability of decentralized protests to adapt and persist despite significant challenges.

- *Formation of Broad-Based Government:* In response to widespread protests and political unrest that lasted about a month, President William Ruto dismissed his entire cabinet in July 2024 and proposed the formation of a broad-based government. This approach aimed to include representatives from various political factions and stakeholders to address the grievances of the protesters, particularly the youth. The broad-based government was seen as a step towards inclusive governance, promoting national unity and reducing the likelihood of further unrest. However, some critics argued that it risked undermining democratic principles by blurring the lines between the government and opposition.
- *Rising Abductions of Youths:* Kenya has experienced a troubling rise in the abductions of youths, particularly those involved in political dissent and protests. Since June 2024, many young people have gone missing, creating a climate of fear and uncertainty. These abductions have mainly been linked to state security agencies, with unconfirmed organized crime, or terrorist groups. The government's response has been criticized for lacking transparency and accountability, further eroding public trust. The abductions have sparked further protests and calls for justice, highlighting the ongoing struggle for freedom and security in Kenya.

Nigeria:

#EndSARS Movement

The #EndSARS movement in Nigeria highlighted the issue of police brutality and abductions. Despite the disbandment of the Special Anti-Robbery Squad (SARS), reports of abductions and disappearances continue to surface, particularly targeting activists and protesters. The movement, characterized by its decentralized leadership, successfully pressured the government to disband SARS and address broader issues of police reform. The movement's use of social media to organize protests and share information played a crucial role in its success.

This, too, had a significant impact on Nigerian politics. It highlighted deep-rooted structural issues within the country, including corruption, impunity, and the need for police reform. The widespread participation and solidarity displayed during the protest signaled a growing voice of Nigerian youth in demanding accountability from the government. The protest also sparked a discussion on the role of the international community in addressing human rights violations. The increased political consciousness and mobilization among Nigerian youths have led to greater political engagement and participation, with many young Nigerians becoming more politically active and involved in governance.

#EndBadGovernance Protests

In 2024, the #EndBadGovernance protests emerged in Nigeria, after Kenya's GenZ protests, driven by similar prevalent dissatisfaction with government corruption and economic hardship. The decentralized nature of the protests enabled widespread participation and adaptability, making it challenging for the government to suppress the movement. Protesters used social media platforms to coordinate actions, share updates, and mobilize support, demonstrating the power of collective action in challenging systemic issues.

South Africa:
#FeesMustFall
The Fees Must Fall movement in South Africa, which began in 2015, was a student-led protest against the increase in university fees. The movement, characterized by its decentralized leadership, successfully pressured the government to freeze fee increases and address broader issues of inequality in higher education. The movement's ability to sustain momentum and adapt to changing circumstances highlighted the strengths of leaderless leadership.

- *Youth Resilience and Leaderless Revolution:* The youth-led protests in South Africa, such as the *1976 Soweto Uprising*, have historically demonstrated the power of leaderless movements. More recently, the *Activate Change Drivers Network*, a leaderless revolution comprising over four thousand young people, has been working towards positive change in their communities. This network exemplifies how resilient youth can collaborate for societal good without a single leader.

Bangladesh:
In 2024, Bangladesh experienced significant political unrest, changeover and youth-led protests demanding reform of a controversial quota system for government jobs. The movement, characterized by its decentralized leadership, saw students and youth activists at the forefront, using social media to coordinate actions and amplify their message. Despite facing state repression, including an eight-day internet shutdown, the protesters persisted in their demands for change.

This scenario in Bangladesh mirrors the dynamics of leaderless movements, highlighting the power of collective action and the challenges of maintaining momentum amidst state repression.

United States

#BlackLivesMatter

The Black Lives Matter (BLM) movement, founded in 2013, has had a profound impact on the global conversation about race and justice. BLM has brought attention to systemic racism and police brutality, inspiring similar movements worldwide. The decentralized structure of BLM has enabled it to adapt and grow, despite facing significant challenges. The movement has successfully shifted the national conversation about policing and has influenced policy changes, such as the firing of police chiefs and the closure of detention facilities.

The movement was founded in 2013 by three radical Black organizers—Alicia Garza, Patrisse Cullors, and Opal Tometi—in response to the acquittal of George Zimmerman, who was charged with the murder of Trayvon Martin. The movement gained national recognition following the 2014 deaths of Michael Brown in Ferguson, Missouri, and Eric Garner in New York City. BLM has since grown into a global movement advocating for racial justice and police reform, with chapters in various countries.

- *Implications for Future Leadership*
- *Political Implications:* Leaderless movements are reshaping political systems and leadership styles in Kenya and beyond. The success of movements like #OccupyParliament, #OccupyChurches and #OccupyJKIA demonstrates the potential for collective action to drive significant change. These movements challenge traditional hierarchical structures and promote more inclusive and participatory approaches to governance.
- *Future Trends:* Looking ahead, leaderless leadership is likely to continue influencing various sectors. As technology advances and social media becomes more integral to organizing and mobilizing, the principles of leaderless leadership will play a crucial role in shaping future movements and inspiring change.

- *Youth Activism:* Youth activism is being profoundly influenced by leaderless movements. Young people are leveraging social media to organize and mobilize, bypassing traditional structures and creating new avenues for political engagement. This has led to increased political participation among youth, who are now at the forefront of advocating for social justice, climate action, and economic reform.
- *Social Media Influence:* Social media has become a powerful tool for leaderless movements, enabling rapid communication, organization, and mobilization. Platforms like Twitter, Facebook, and Instagram allow activists to share information, coordinate actions, and amplify their messages to a global audience. This has democratized activism, allowing anyone with internet access to participate and contribute.

➢ *Case Study: ADANI Group and JKIA Protests*

The proposed takeover of Nairobi's Jomo Kenyatta International Airport (JKIA) by India's Adani Group triggered widespread protests in Kenya. The deal, which involved a USD 1.85 billion investment by Adani in exchange for the operation of the airport for 30 years, among other hidden details, raised concerns about the privatization of a critical national asset. The protests reflect broader anxieties about foreign investment in strategic national assets and highlight the importance of transparency and public involvement in decision-making processes.

- *Inclusivity and Participatory Governance*
- *Parliamentary vs. Presidential System:* The quest for political inclusivity in Kenya has sparked debates about whether the country should adopt a parliamentary system in place of its current presidential system. A parliamentary system may offer greater inclusivity and participatory governance by ensuring that the executive branch is accountable to the legislative body,

which represents a broader spectrum of the population. This can help avert negative ethnicity, skewed developments, and rampant mega grand corruption by promoting a more balanced and representative government. On the other hand, a presidential system can provide a strong and stable leadership, but it may also concentrate power in the hands of a single individual, potentially leading to abuses of power and less accountability.

- ✓ Parliamentary System:
  In a parliamentary system, the executive branch is derived from the legislative body, and the head of government (Prime Minister) is elected from among the members of parliament. This system promotes a closer relationship between the executive and legislative branches, allowing for more coordinated policy-making. It can enhance inclusivity and participatory governance by ensuring that the government reflects the composition of the parliament. However, it can also lead to instability if the régime loses the confidence of the parliament.

- ✓ Presidential System:
  In a presidential system, the President is directly elected by the people and serves as both the head of state and the head of government. This system provides a clear separation of powers between the executive, legislative, and judicial branches, promoting checks and balances. It can offer stability and a strong mandate for the President. However, it can also lead to gridlock if there is significant opposition between the executive and legislative branches.

- *Youth Involvement in Politics Post-Protests*
- Kenya: Post-Protest Political Engagement: Following the #OccupyParliament, #OccupyChurches and #OccupyJKIA movements, there has been a noticeable increase in political engagement among Kenyan youth. Many young people who participated in these protests have continued to be active in political discourse, advocating for policy changes and greater accountability from their leaders. The protests have also led to the formation of youth-led organizations and initiatives aimed at addressing social and economic issues. This increased political consciousness among the youth is fostering a new generation of leaders who are committed to driving change from within the system.
- Nigeria: Impact of #EndSARS on Youth Political Engagement: The #EndSARS movement had a profound impact on youth political engagement in Nigeria. The protests highlighted the power of collective action and the importance of holding government officials accountable. In the aftermath of the protests, many young Nigerians have become more politically active, participating in voter registration drives, running for political office, and engaging in community organizing. The movement also led to the establishment of various youth-led advocacy groups focused on police reform, human rights, and good governance. The increased political participation among Nigerian youth is a testament to the lasting impact of the #EndSARS movement on the country's political landscape.
- South Africa: Youth Resilience and Political Involvement: In South Africa, the Fees Must Fall movement and other youth-led protests have led to greater political involvement among young people. The success of these movements has inspired many

young South Africans to engage in political activism and advocacy. Youth-led organizations and networks, such as the Activate Change Drivers Network, continue to work towards positive change in their communities, addressing issues such as education, employment, and social justice. The resilience and determination of South African youth in the face of adversity have made them key players in the country's political landscape.

- *Statistics About Protest Outcomes*

According to the *Global Protest Tracker by the Carnegie Endowment for International Peace*, over 800 significant anti-government protests have erupted worldwide since 2017, with more than 150 countries experiencing significant protests. Approximately 18% of these protests have lasted more than three months, and 283 significant economic anti-government protests have occurred during this period. *The Nonviolent and Violent Campaigns and Outcomes (NAVCO) Data Project* also provides comprehensive data on the characteristics and outcomes of resistance campaigns globally, covering 627 mass mobilizations from 1900 to 2021.

- *Conclusion*

Leaderless movements represent a new paradigm in modern politics. By empowering voices and fostering creativity, these movements have demonstrated the potential for collective action to drive significant change. The examples from Kenya, Nigeria, South Africa, Bangladesh and the global Black Lives Matter movement illustrate how decentralized leadership can effectively challenge systemic issues and inspire widespread participation.

The implications for future leadership are profound. As technology advances and social media becomes more integral to organizing and mobilizing, the principles of leaderless leadership will continue to shape political systems and movements. Youth activism, in particular, is being transformed by these movements, with young people leveraging digital platforms to advocate for social justice, climate action, and economic reforms.

CHAPTER 25:
The Integrity of Right and Wrong

In the journey of leaderless leadership, one fundamental principle stands out: the unwavering commitment to doing what is right, even when it is difficult or unpopular. This principle is encapsulated in the saying, "What's wrong is wrong, even if everyone does it, and what's right is right, even if no one does it."

This concept underscores the importance of moral integrity and ethical decision-making in all aspects of leadership. "The time is always right to do what is right" (King, 1963). "Do not follow the crowd in doing wrong. When you give testimony in a lawsuit, do not pervert justice by siding with the crowd." (Exodus 23:2, NIV)

- *The Importance of Moral Integrity*

Moral integrity involves adhering to ethical principles and values, regardless of external pressures or societal norms. It requires a steadfast commitment to doing what is right, even when it is challenging or goes against the grain. In leaderless leadership, moral integrity is crucial for maintaining trust, credibility, and the ethical foundation of the organization or movement. As Aldo Leopold aptly put it, "Ethical behavior is doing what's right when no one is watching – even when doing wrong is legal" (Leopold, n.d.).

- *The Principle of "What's Wrong is Wrong, Even if Everyone Does It"*

This principle emphasizes the importance of adhering to ethical standards and moral integrity, regardless of external influences or societal pressures. It is a call to maintain one's values and principles, even when faced with widespread acceptance of unethical behavior.

- *The Challenge of Conformity:* In many situations, individuals may feel pressured to conform to the actions and beliefs of the majority. This can be particularly challenging when the majority engages in unethical practices. The principle that "what's wrong is wrong, even if everyone does it" serves as a reminder to resist the temptation to follow the crowd and to stand firm in one's convictions.

For example, in corporate settings, employees may encounter situations where unethical practices, such as falsifying reports or engaging in corrupt activities, are normalized. Despite the pressure to conform, it is crucial to recognize that these actions are wrong and to take a stand against them. This commitment to ethical behavior helps maintain the integrity of the organization and fosters a culture of trust and accountability.

- *Ethical Decision-Making*

Ethical decision-making is at the heart of leaderless leadership. It involves evaluating actions and decisions based on their alignment with core values and ethical principles. This process requires critical thinking, self-awareness, and a commitment to the greater good. By prioritizing ethical considerations, leaderless organizations can ensure that their actions reflect their values and contribute to positive social change. As the Bible states, "Whoever can be trusted with very little can also be trusted with much, and whoever is dishonest with very little will also be dishonest with much" (Luke 16:10, NIV).

- *Historical Examples*

Throughout history, there have been numerous instances where individuals and groups have stood up against widespread wrongdoing, often at great personal risk. These examples serve as powerful reminders of the importance of moral integrity.

- Case Studies
- Political Governance
- ✓ The Civil Rights Movement

The Civil Rights Movement in the United States is a powerful example of the principle that "what's right is right, even if no one does it." Leaders like Martin Luther King Jr. and countless activists stood up against systemic racism and injustice, often facing significant opposition and personal risk. Their unwavering commitment to justice and equality, even in the face of widespread resistance, ultimately led to transformative social change. As Martin Luther King Jr. famously said, "Injustice anywhere is a threat to justice everywhere" (King, 1963).

- ✓ Governance in South Africa

Post-apartheid South Africa provides a compelling case study in political governance. The transition from apartheid to a democratic government was marked by significant challenges, including the need to address past injustices and build a new, inclusive political system. The Truth and Reconciliation Commission (TRC), led by Archbishop Desmond Tutu, exemplified the principle that "what's right is right, even if no one does it." The TRC's work in uncovering the truth about human rights violations and promoting reconciliation was crucial in laying the foundation for a more just and equitable society (Tutu, 1999).

- ✓ Gender-Based Participation in Kenya and Uganda

In Kenya and Uganda, efforts to increase gender-based participation in political institutions highlight the importance of ethical decision-making in governance. Despite the challenges, both countries have made strides in promoting gender equality through affirmative action and legislative reforms. These efforts underscore the principle that "what's right is right, even if no one does it," as they aim to create more inclusive and representative political systems (Kiarie, 2016).

- Corporate Governance
  - ✓ Ghanaian Financial Institutions

A study on the application of corporate governance practices in the banking sector of Ghana revealed the importance of transparency and accountability. The research highlighted the need for adequate disclosure and compliance with regulatory requirements to ensure good governance. This case study underscores the principle that "what's right is right, even if no one does it," as it emphasizes the importance of ethical practices in maintaining trust and stability in the financial sector (Campion et al., 2022).

- ✓ Nigerian Corporate Governance

In Nigeria, corporate governance has been a critical issue, particularly in the wake of financial scandals and corporate failures. Efforts to improve governance practices have focused on enhancing transparency, accountability, and stakeholder engagement. These reforms are essential for building trust and ensuring the long-term sustainability of businesses. The principle that "what's right is right, even if no one does it" is central to these efforts, as it highlights the need for ethical leadership and decision-making (AfDB, 2007).

- *The Role of Personal Integrity*

Personal integrity plays a crucial role in upholding the principle that "what's wrong is wrong, even if everyone does it." It involves being true to one's values and principles, even in the face of adversity. This requires courage, self-awareness, and a strong sense of moral responsibility.

In everyday life, individuals may encounter situations where they must choose between doing what is right and conforming to the actions of others. For example, a student may witness cheating during an exam and feel pressured to join in. However, adhering to the principle that "what's wrong is wrong" means resisting this pressure and choosing to act with integrity.

- *Practical Applications*

To apply this principle in daily life, consider the following steps:

- *Reflect on Your Values:* Regularly reflect on your core values and ensure your actions align with them.
- *Seek Accountability:* Surround yourself with people who will hold you accountable to your ethical standards.
- *Practice Empathy:* Consider the impact of your decisions on others and strive to act with compassion and fairness.
- *Stay Informed:* Educate yourself on ethical principles and stay informed about current ethical issues.
- *Lead by Example:* Demonstrate ethical behavior in your daily actions and decisions, inspiring others to do the same.

- *Counterarguments to the Principle*

While the principle of "what's wrong is wrong, even if everyone does it" is widely upheld, there are counterarguments that challenge its application:

- *Cultural Relativism:* Some argue that moral standards are not universal and can vary significantly across cultures. What is considered wrong in one culture may be acceptable in another, making it difficult to apply a single ethical standard universally (Pijanowski, 2009).
- *Situational Ethics:* This perspective suggests that the context of a situation can influence what is considered right or wrong. Proponents argue that rigid adherence to moral principles may not always be practical or beneficial, and ethical decisions should be made based on the specific circumstances (Scholl et al., 2018).
- *Moral Complexity:* Ethical dilemmas often involve complex situations where multiple values and principles are at stake. In such cases, determining what is right or wrong may not be straightforward, and

individuals may need to balance competing ethical considerations (Scholl et al., 2018).

- *Pragmatism:* Some argue that ethical decision-making should be guided by practical considerations and the potential outcomes of actions. This approach emphasizes the importance of achieving the best possible results, even if it means compromising on certain moral principles (Scholl et al., 2018).

- *The Role of Collective Conscience*

In leaderless movements, the collective conscience of the group plays a vital role in guiding ethical behavior. This shared sense of right and wrong helps to ensure that decisions and actions align with the movement's values and principles. By fostering a culture of ethical awareness and mutual accountability, leaderless organizations can navigate complex moral dilemmas and maintain their integrity.

- *Overcoming Ethical Challenges*

Leaderless organizations may face ethical challenges, such as pressure to conform to unethical practices or the temptation to compromise values for short-term gains. To overcome these challenges, it is essential to:

- *Reinforce Core Values:* Regularly revisit and reaffirm the organization's core values and ethical principles. This helps to keep them at the forefront of decision-making processes.
- *Encourage Open Dialogue:* Create an environment where members feel comfortable discussing ethical concerns and dilemmas. Open dialogue fosters mutual understanding and collective problem-solving.
- *Lead by Example:* Members should model ethical behavior in their actions and decisions. Leading by example reinforces the importance of integrity and sets a standard for others to follow.
- *Hold Each Other Accountable:* Establish mechanisms for mutual accountability, where members can respectfully

challenge and support each other in upholding ethical standards.

Barbara Grizzuti Harrison noted, "The most painful moral struggles are not those between good and evil, but between the good and the lesser good" (Harrison, 1989).

- *Common Ethical Dilemmas*

Ethical dilemmas arise when individuals must choose between conflicting moral principles. Some common ethical dilemmas include:

- *Truth vs. Loyalty:* Choosing between being honest and being loyal to a person or organization. For example, an employee may discover fraudulent activities within their company and must decide whether to report it (truth) or remain loyal to their colleagues (loyalty) (Markkula Center for Applied Ethics, n.d.).
- *Individual vs. Community:* Balancing personal interests with the needs of the community. During a pandemic, individuals may resist wearing masks for personal comfort, but this conflicts with the community's need for public safety (Markkula Center for Applied Ethics, n.d.).
- *Short-term vs. Long-term:* Deciding between immediate benefits and long-term consequences. A business might cut corners to make profits now, despite potential long-term damage to its reputation (Markkula Center for Applied Ethics, n.d.).
- *Justice vs. Mercy:* Weighing fair consequences against compassion. A judge might struggle with issuing a strict sentence (justice) or showing leniency (mercy) to a first-time offender (Markkula Center for Applied Ethics, n.d.).

Georg Wilhelm Friedrich Hegel observed, "Genuine tragedies in the world are not conflicts between right and wrong. They are conflicts between two rights" (Hegel, n.d.).

- *Scriptural Guidance*

The Bible offers timeless wisdom on ethical behavior and decision-making:

- ✓ "Do to others as you would have them do to you." (Luke 6:31, NIV)
- ✓ "The integrity of the upright guides them, but the unfaithful are destroyed by their duplicity." (Proverbs 11:3, NIV)
- ✓ "Whatever you do, work at it with all your heart, as working for the Lord, not for human masters." (Colossians 3:23, NIV)

- *Applying These Principles in Daily Life:* To apply these principles in daily life, consider the following steps:
- ✓ Reflect on Your Values: Regularly reflect on your core values and ensure your actions align with them.
- ✓ Seek Accountability: Surround yourself with people who will hold you accountable to your ethical standards.
- ✓ Practice Empathy: Consider the impact of your decisions on others and strive to act with compassion and fairness.
- ✓ Stay Informed: Educate yourself on ethical principles and stay informed about current ethical issues.
- ✓ Lead by Example: Demonstrate ethical behavior in your daily actions and decisions, inspiring others to do the same.
- ✓ Humorous Quote: "Why did the deontologist refuse to play hide and seek? Because they believed hiding would violate the categorical imperative!" (Havens, 2023).

- *How Humor Enhances Ethical Discussions*

Humor can be a powerful tool in ethical discussions. It can break down barriers, making difficult conversations more approachable and engaging. By using humor, we can highlight the absurdity of unethical behavior and encourage reflection on moral principles in a lighthearted yet impactful way. Humor also fosters a sense of camaraderie and openness, which can lead to more honest and productive discussions about ethics (Benatar, 2024).

- *Final Thoughts*

In the realm of leaderless leadership, the commitment to doing what is right, regardless of external influences, is a cornerstone of ethical and effective leadership. By upholding moral integrity and fostering a culture of ethical decision-making, leaderless organizations can inspire trust, drive positive change, and create a more just and equitable world. Albert Einstein wisely noted, "You can't resolve a dilemma with all the very same mind that made it" (Einstein, n.d.).

CHAPTER 26:
The End

"The greatest leader is not necessarily the one who does the greatest things. (S)He is the one that gets the people to do the greatest things."

— Ronald Reagan

As we conclude our exploration of leaderless leadership, it is clear that this model offers a transformative approach to organizing and leading groups. By examining the principles, mechanics, ethical considerations, and real-world applications of leaderless leadership, we can appreciate its potential to create more inclusive, innovative, and resilient organizations and nations.

- *The Power of Inclusivity and Equal Participation*

Leaderless leadership emphasizes the importance of inclusivity and equal participation. By ensuring that every member has a voice in decision-making processes, leaderless organizations foster a sense of ownership and responsibility. This inclusivity not only enriches the decision-making process but also promotes a culture of mutual respect and collaboration. As highlighted in the *Occupy Wall Street* movement, diverse voices and perspectives can drive significant social change.

- *Transparency and Accountability*

Transparency and accountability are cornerstones of ethical leaderless leadership. Open communication and shared responsibility ensure that all members are informed and accountable for their actions. This transparency builds trust and fosters a collaborative environment where members feel valued and empowered. The Mondragon Corporation exemplifies how transparency and accountability can drive organizational success and resilience.

- *Ethical Decision-Making and Conflict Resolution*

Ethical decision-making and effective conflict resolution are crucial for maintaining harmony and integrity in leaderless organizations. Consensus-building techniques and conflict resolution mechanisms, such as mediation and restorative circles, ensure that decisions reflect the collective will and ethical standards of the group. The Zapatista movement and the Pirate Party demonstrate how these practices can foster a culture of trust and mutual support.

- *Empowerment and Trust*

Empowerment and trust are fundamental to the success of leaderless leadership. By empowering members to take initiative and contribute their skills, leaderless organizations foster a sense of ownership and responsibility. Trust is built through transparency, open communication, and a commitment to ethical principles. The Linux open-source community and various tech startups illustrate how empowerment and trust can drive innovation and collaboration.

- *Ethical Sustainability and Long-Term Vision*

Ethical sustainability involves considering the long-term impact of the organization's actions on the community and environment. Leaderless organizations prioritize sustainability by making decisions that balance economic, social, and environmental considerations. The Mondragon Corporation and Patagonia are examples of how ethical sustainability can drive business success and positively impact society.

- *The Role of Technology and Social Media*

Technology and social media are shaping the future of leaderless leadership. AI and blockchain enhance decision-making processes and ensure transparency, while social media platforms enable rapid mobilization and coordination of efforts. These technologies empower leaderless organizations to operate more efficiently and effectively, as seen in Decentralized Autonomous Organizations (DAOs) and various social movements.

- *Preparing for the Future*

To thrive in leaderless organizations and societies, individuals need to develop specific skills and mindsets, including adaptability, collaboration, and a commitment to continuous learning. Educational institutions and organizations must provide training programs that equip individuals with these skills. Policymakers should consider regulations and incentives that support leaderless structures, recognizing their potential to drive innovation and societal change.

- *Let's Change Poor Politics and End Bad Governance*

As we stand on the precipice of a new era, the words of Angela Davis resonate deeply: *"You have to act as if it were possible to radically transform the world. And you have to do it all the time."* This relentless commitment to change is the heartbeat of leaderless movements. They remind us that true power lies not in the hands of a single charismatic leader but in the collective strength of many voices united by a common purpose for the common societal good.

Leaderless movements have shown us that positive change is possible when we come together, empowered by our shared goals and diverse perspectives. From the Arab Spring to the Black Lives Matter movement, these decentralized efforts have demonstrated the power of collective action in challenging the status quo and driving meaningful societal shifts.

In the words of Martin Luther King Jr., *"Injustice anywhere is a threat to justice everywhere."* This timeless truth underscores the importance of continuous, collective effort in the fight for justice and equality. By embracing the principles of leaderless leadership, we can create a more inclusive and participatory future, where every voice is heard, and every individual has the power to make a difference.

- *Holy Scriptures*

The Bible also offers profound insights into the power of collective action and the importance of *moving forward with faith and courage.* Joshua 1:9 reminds us, *"Have I not commanded you? Be strong and courageous. Do not be afraid; do not be discouraged, for the Lord your God will be with you wherever you go."* This verse encourages us to step out in faith, knowing that we are not alone in our journey towards meaningful change.

Similarly, Proverbs 4:12 assure us, *"When you walk, your steps will not be hampered; when you run, you will not stumble."* This promise of divine guidance and protection reinforces the idea that when we align our actions with a higher purpose, we can move forward with confidence and resilience.

- *Resilience in Tough Times*

In recent years, Bangladesh has witnessed the power of leaderless movements. The youth-led protests in 2024 against the controversial quota system for government jobs exemplify the strength of collective action. Despite facing significant challenges, including state repression and an internet shutdown, the protesters persisted, demonstrating the resilience and determination that define leaderless movements.

- *Fruitful Future*

As we look into the future, let us draw inspiration from these movements and the *timeless wisdom of scripture.* Let us embrace the power of collective leadership, knowing that together, we can create a world that is more just, inclusive, and compassionate. By acting as if it were possible to radically transform the world, and doing so with unwavering commitment, we can indeed inspire change and empower voices for generations to come.

- *Final Thoughts*

Leaderless leadership offers a powerful and transformative approach to organizing and leading groups. By embracing the principles of inclusivity, transparency, ethical decision-making, empowerment, and sustainability, leaderless organizations can create more equitable and resilient environments. As we move forward, the principles of leaderless leadership will continue to shape organizations and societies, fostering a more inclusive, innovative, and sustainable world. Thank you for embarking on this journey of exploration and reflection. May this book serve as a beacon of hope and a call to action for all who seek to make a difference in our world.

APPENDICES

Resources and Further Reading

Books:

1. Akanbi, P. A., & Ofoegbu, O. E. (2013). A Model of Virtuous Leadership in Africa: Case Study of a Nigerian Firm.
2. Bacon, J., 2012. The Art of Community: Building the New Age of Participation. Sebastopol: O'Reilly Media.
3. Benatar, D. (2024). Taking Humour (Ethics) Seriously, But Not Too Seriously. Journal of Practical Ethics.
4. Brafman, O. and Beckstrom, R.A. (2006). The Starfish and the Spider: The Unstoppable Power of Leaderless Organizations. New York: Penguin Group.
5. Campion, C. B., Aduamoah, M., Amoah, R. A., & Marfo, I. O. (2022). Corporate Governance Practices in Ghanaian Financial Institutions.
6. Chouinard, Y., 2005. Let My People Go Surfing: The Education of a Reluctant Businessman. New York: Penguin Books.
7. Harrison, B. G. (1989). The Struggle for Moral Integrity.
8. Havens, J. (2023). 6 Hilarious Ethical Quandaries for Ethics Awareness Month.
9. Hegel, G. W. F. (n.d.). Ethical Dilemmas Quotes.
10. Kiarie, W. (2016). Gender-Based Participation in Political Institutions in Kenya and Uganda.
11. King, M. L. Jr. (1963). Letter from Birmingham Jail.
12. Laloux, F., 2014. Reinventing Organizations: A Guide to Creating Organizations Inspired by the Next Stage of Human Consciousness. Brussels: Nelson Parker.
13. Leopold, A. (n.d.). Inspiring Ethics Quotes: On Moral Values and Integrity.
14. Markkula Center for Applied Ethics. (n.d.). Ethics in Everyday Life: Practical Guide to Moral Decisions.
15. Pijanowski, J. (2009). Analysis of Barriers to Effective Moral Decision Making.

16. Pink, D.H., 2009. Drive: The Surprising Truth About What Motivates Us. New York: Riverhead Books.
17. Ries, E., 2011. The Lean Startup: How Today's Entrepreneurs Use Continuous Innovation to Create Radically Successful Businesses. New York: Crown Business.
18. Ross, C. (2011). The Leaderless Revolution: How Ordinary People Will Take Power and Change Politics in the 21st Century. New York: Blue Rider Press.
19. Scholl, J. A., Mederer, H. J., & Scholl, R. W. (2018). Leadership, Ethics, and Decision-Making.
20. Sinek, S. (2009). Start with Why: How Great Leaders Inspire Everyone to Take Action. New York: Penguin Group.
21. Tutu, D. (1999). No Future Without Forgiveness.
22. Wambugu, P. (2014). African Culture and School Leadership: A Case Study of Secondary School Leaders in Kenya.

Articles:

1. Bourke, J. and Espedido, A., 2020. Why Inclusive Leaders Are Good for Organizations, and How to Become One. Harvard Business Review, [online] Available at: https://hbr.org/2020/03/why-inclusive-leaders-are-good-for-organizations-and-how-to-become-one [Accessed 30 December 2024].
2. Harvard Business Review. (2021). "The Future of Leadership: 10 Ways Leaders Can Thrive in the Future of Work." Available at: Forbes.
3. Khan Academy, 2024. Khan Academy. [online] Available at: https://www.khanacademy.org [Accessed 30 December 2024].
4. Korn Ferry. (2025). "Top 5 Leadership Trends That Will Shape 2025." Available at: Korn Ferry
5. Narayanan, A., Bonneau, J., Felten, E., Miller, A. and Goldfeder, S., 2016. Blockchain Technology: Principles and Applications. Foundations and Trends in Information and Technology, 2(1), pp.1-156.

6. Quantic Blog. (2022). "The Future of Leadership in 2030: 6 New Disruptive Trends." Available at: Quantic
7. Senge, P., Hamilton, H. and Kania, J., 2015. The Dawn of System Leadership. Harvard Business Review, [online] Available at: https://hbr.org/2015/01/the-dawn-of-system-leadership [Accessed 30 December 2024].

Websites:

1. Ethereum, 2024. Ethereum. [online] Available at: https://www.ethereum.org [Accessed 30 December 2024].
2. HR Katha. (2024). "Can the future of workplaces be leaderless?" Available at: HR Katha
3. Khan Academy, 2024. Khan Academy. [online] Available at: https://www.khanacademy.org [Accessed 30 December 2024].
4. Linux Foundation, 2024. Linux Foundation. [online] Available at: https://www.linuxfoundation.org [Accessed 30 December 2024].
5. Mondragon Corporation. (2024). "Our Principles." Available at: Mondragon Corporation
6. Patagonia, 2024. Patagonia. [online] Available at: https://www.patagonia.com [Accessed 30 December 2024].
7. Police1. (2024). "Could law enforcement be leader-LESS in the future?" Available at: Police1
8. TED, 2024. TED Talks. [online] Available at: https://www.ted.com [Accessed 30 December 2024].

These resources should provide a comprehensive foundation for understanding and applying the principles of leaderless leadership. Enjoy exploring these materials!

Tools and Platforms for Leaderless Collaboration

Collaboration Platforms

1. Slack: A messaging app for teams that brings all communication together, creating a more connected and productive workspace.
2. Microsoft Teams: A collaboration platform that combines persistent workplace chat, video meetings, file storage, and application integration.
3. Trello: A web-based project management application that uses boards, lists, and cards to organize tasks and projects.

Decision-Making Tools

1. Loomio: A decision-making tool designed to assist groups with collaborative decision-making processes.
2. Pol.is: A real-time system for gathering, analyzing, and understanding what large groups of people think in their own words.

Document Sharing

1. Google Drive: A file storage and synchronization service that allows users to store files in the cloud, synchronize files across devices, and share files.
2. Dropbox: A file hosting service that offers cloud storage, file synchronization, personal cloud, and client software.

Virtual Meeting Tools

1. Zoom: A video conferencing tool that provides remote conferencing services using cloud computing.
2. Microsoft Teams: Also serves as a virtual meeting tool, enabling remote collaboration and regular check-ins.

INTERVIEWS AND TESTIMONIALS

Insights from Experts and Practitioners

1. Carne Ross: Author of The Leaderless Revolution, Ross discusses the power of ordinary people to take control and effect change without traditional leadership structures.
2. Ori Brafman: Co-author of The Starfish and the Spider, Brafman explores the dynamics of decentralized organizations and how they can thrive without a central leader.

Personal Stories from Leaderless Leaders

1. Linux Contributors: Stories from developers who contribute to the Linux open-source project, highlighting their experiences with collaborative decision-making and innovation.
2. Zapatista Community Members: Testimonials from members of the Zapatista movement, sharing their experiences with collective governance and community empowerment.

Glossary

1. Blockchain: A decentralized digital ledger that records transactions across many computers so that the record cannot be altered retroactively.
2. Consensus Building: A process of decision-making that seeks the agreement of most participants.
3. Decentralized Autonomous Organization (DAO): An organization represented by rules encoded as a computer program that is transparent, controlled by organization members, and not influenced by a central government.
4. Holacracy: A method of decentralized management and organizational governance in which authority and decision-making are distributed throughout a holarchy of self-organizing teams.

5. Inclusivity: The practice or policy of including people who might otherwise be excluded or marginalized.
6. Participatory Budgeting: A process of democratic deliberation and decision-making in which ordinary people decide how to allocate part of a municipal or public budget.
7. Restorative Circles: A conflict resolution process that brings together those who have a stake in a conflict to collectively resolve it and repair harm.

References

1. Brafman, O. and Beckstrom, R.A., 2006. The Starfish and the Spider: The Unstoppable Power of Leaderless Organizations. New York: Penguin Group.
2. Forbes, 2021. "The Future of Leadership: 10 Ways Leaders Can Thrive In The Future Of Work." Available at: https://www.forbes.com/sites/glennllopis/2021/12/06/the-future-of-leadership-10-ways-leaders-can-thrive-in-the-future-of-work/ [Accessed 10 October 2024].
3. Galatians 3:28, New International Version.
4. Harvard Business Review, 2021. "The Future of Leadership: 10 Ways Leaders Can Thrive in the Future of Work." Available at: https://www.forbes.com/sites/glennllopis/2021/12/06/the-future-of-leadership-10-ways-leaders-can-thrive-in-the-future-of-work/ [Accessed 10 October 2024].
5. Hebrews 10:25, New International Version.
6. HR Katha, 2024. "Can the future of workplaces be leaderless?" Available at: https://www.hrkatha.com/features/can-the-future-of-workplaces-be-leaderless/ [Accessed 10 October 2024].
7. Korn Ferry, 2025. "Top 5 Leadership Trends That Will Shape 2025." Available at: https://www.kornferry.com/insights/featured-topics/leadership/top-5-leadership-trends-2025 [Accessed 10 October 2024].
8. Mondragon Corporation, 2024. "Our Principles." Available: https://www.mondragoncorporation.com/en/about-us/our-principles/ [Accessed 10 October 2024].
9. Police1, 2024. "Could law enforcement be leader-LESS in the future?" Available at:

https://www.police1.com/chiefs-sheriffs/articles/could-law-enforcement-be-leader-less-in-the-future/ [Accessed 10 October 2024].

10. Proverbs 11:14, New International Version.
11. Proverbs 15:22, New International Version.
12. Proverbs 27:17, New International Version.
13. Quantic Blog, 2022. "The Future of Leadership in 2030: 6 New Disruptive Trends." Available at: https://quantic.edu/blog/2022/08/05/the-future-of-leadership-in-2030-6-new-disruptive-trends/ [Accessed 10 October 2024].
14. Ross, C., 2011. The Leaderless Revolution: How Ordinary People Will Take Power and Change Politics in the 21st Century. New York: Blue Rider Press.
15. Sinek, S., 2009. Start with Why: How Great Leaders Inspire Everyone to Take Action. New York: Penguin Group.

ABOUT THE AUTHOR

Pastor Ochieng is a man who seamlessly blends faith, finance, and leadership into a tapestry of wisdom and inspiration.

A born-again Christian and a Five-Fold Minister, he currently serves as an Associate Pastor at Rock Fellowship Ministries, Church on The Rock / Africa Churches on The Rock & Christian Ministries in Africa Headquarters in Karen, Nairobi, Kenya.

Happily married to the lovely Cate Cherop, together they have built a blessed family that stands as a testament to their faith and love.

An alumnus of Moi University, School of Business and Economics, Class of 2011, Pastor majored in Finance and Banking. He is a proud member of the Institute of Public Accountants of Kenya (ICPAK) and the Kenya Institute of Management (KIM). He brings a wealth of experience to his role as an Audit Manager at Crowe Erastus & Co., Nairobi, Kenya, and an esteemed member firm of Crowe Global. His expertise spans accounting, finance, audit, management, and leadership orientation.

His journey through life has been a rich tapestry of lessons on moral values and leadership. His passion for embracing meaningful moral behavior and harnessing collective power is evident in his latest book, "The Leaderless Leader: Harnessing Collective Power in a Decentralized World." *He believes that true leadership is not about titles or positions but about empowering others and fostering a sense of community.*

As he often says, "In a world where everyone wants to lead, the true leader is the one who empowers others to find their own path." His book is a testament to this belief, filled with personal anecdotes, humor, and wisdom that resonate deeply with readers. He draws inspiration from scriptures such as Matthew 20:26, "Whoever wants to become great among you must be your servant," *highlighting the essence of servant leadership.*

With a heart for meaningful moral behavior at every level of life, *Pastor Ben's insights are both profound and practical.* His engaging writing style, combined with his deep faith and professional experience, makes this book a must-read for anyone looking to lead in a decentralized world.

Pastor Ochieng can be contacted at:

Mobile – +254 763 109 067
Email Address – info@bensbestbooks.com and bensbestbooks2025@gmail.com
Website – www.bensbestbooks.com